D1015190

COLD NOSES
AT
THE PEARLY GATES

A BOOK OF HOPE

BY: GARY KURZ

Library of Congress Cataloging in Publication Data
Txu 797-590
Kurz, Gary
Cold Noses at the Pearly Gates

Second Edition, December 2002

All material and pictures were provided by the author unless otherwise acknowledged.

Cover artistry by Eric and Linda Kurz

ISBN   0-9666117-0-5

DEDICATION

To the many pet friends I have known, who shared portions of my life and all of my heart - **Tinkerbell, Scooter, Miko, Fuji, Samantha** and **Pebbles.** You have all gone on ahead. I will catch up to you later.

The years may seem to slowly pass
Memories may begin to wane
The time we long for will come at last
When we shall be together again

Dad

TABLE OF CONTENTS

FOREWORD

Who can one turn to when the unexpected suddenly happens and their long-time pet is no more? Where can they go for help? Often, these things happen without warning and so abruptly that there isn't even time to say goodbye to our wonderful best friends. Even if it is expected, it is still crushing and seems so final. It is as if we are in a bad dream that we cannot awaken from.

There are those learned few psychiatrists and other professionals who stand ready to help us with our trauma and emotions. They are able to assist us to that place of acceptance, and help strengthen our resolve to recover from the blow. But even they cannot mend the broken heart or fill the empty void left in our lives by the irreversible loss.

There is a cure for our hearts however, a way to turn that emptiness into hope...a hope of seeing our pets again. As extraordinary as that may sound, I assure you that it is true. I regret that the circumstances that brought you to this book have occurred in your life, but hope you will find a new joy and hope from the literary journey that you are about to embark upon.

INTRODUCTION

Authors, in a sense, are very similar to inventors. A need must exist in order for their product to be successful. I felt an overwhelming need for a book on the topic of animals and the afterlife. My reasoning was two-fold: first, I needed to know for myself, and there were no books or in-depth writings on this topic; and second, I believed others wanted to know as well.

While researching material for this book, which included the polling of a number of people who represented a cross-section of society, I guardedly disclosed the subject of my research to each of them. I anticipated that there would be a few raised eyebrows. Some where supportive, but most were skeptical, as I had feared. "It will never sell" or "come on...really, what are you writing about?" were generally the type of comments I received. There were other negative comments, but I think those two pretty much sum up the sentiment that was expressed. The consensus was that they did not think the book would be successful.

It was clear to me that our ideas of what constituted success were very different. My idea of success for this book is not that it would be a "cash cow", generating a positive source of income, but rather that it would be a "comfort cow", generating a positive source of help. My motive for writing was singular...I had found comfort and hope in my studies and I knew others could benefit from my discoveries. If only 5 people purchased my book and found the comfort and hope I had found, my book would be a success to me. Production costs would remain far in the red, but my primary goal of helping others would have been achieved.

INTRODUCTION

Although I do not indulge much in infomercial products, I do watch these programs occasionally when sleep is fleeting and I do not feel like reading. On one of those infrequent occasions, a very well-known and successful real estate investor, speaking of his product said "Do not be discouraged by people who will say that you are wasting your time. It is human nature to be negative towards someone who is trying something new and to put them down. You just keep on moving ahead".

His words proved to be so very true in my own undertaking. As soon as those close to me heard I was writing a Biblically-based book on the possibility of animal afterlife, I started drawing negative reviews. And not one word had even been written! To be fair however, looking back, I can see where these people may have mistakenly viewed my work as a "get rich quick" idea rather than the help it is meant to be. In that context, they would probably have been correct.

Fortunately, they incorrectly perceived both my motive and the way the public would receive the book. Many thousands have been helped and comforted over the years and I am so very thankful to have been of service. I am not a licensed counselor, but have been willing to listen and respond to many readers through a special e-mail account I have set up, PETGATE@aol.com. You may also visit our website at www.coldnosesbook.com. It is a work still in progress, but we are trying to help tie together a network of websites whose goals are to help animals and their people.

Simply stated, my reason for writing this book is that pets pass, and when they pass, the people they leave behind grieve. This grief is no less intense than when a human loved one passes.

INTRODUCTION

There is a source of comfort available that is higher than that offered by the many psychology books available on the market today. There is a level of hope and anticipation that most people know absolutely nothing about and my desire is to make them aware of that hope.

In no way do I mean to lessen the worth of the many books that deal with the psychological and emotional recovery process following the loss of a pet. Quite the contrary is true. I have reviewed many of these fine works and found them to be right on the mark in helping people transit the many emotional phases they experience during these tragic and traumatic times.

Indeed, these medical professionals understand the inner workings of our hearts and minds and what it takes to help someone hasten the healing process. Their recovery advice was nothing less than excellent. Time is the great healer, but I believe some of their exercises in rebounding actually speed the healing process in most cases. I would suggest therefore, that anyone who has suffered loss, pet or otherwise, acquire and use one of these books. It will help frame your feelings in a context that will allow you to understand what you are going through and why.

If I find any shortcomings at all in their writings, it would be that:

- despite the great number of books available, I can not recommend one more than the other. They are essentially clones of each other, and while all are good, none are better or worse than the other; and

- while they are very helpful to the individual dealing with grief, they can only offer limited relief. Their final analysis appears to be "get over it and move on".

From a secular point of view, this advice of "closure" makes sense. It is the best natural conclusion that worldly knowledge can offer in regards to loss. I must confess however, that this just is not enough for me. I know I have to get on with my life, and I am. But I really don't want to "get over it". I want to feel better. I want to stop hurting. But I certainly do not want to have closure in the sense some of these professionals intend.

Each of my departed pets left a permanent hole in my heart and a little more emptiness in my life. I love (please note the use of the present tense) each of them and I do not want to forget them at any level. I don't appreciate someone suggesting that I should. Any pet lover would agree that this is just not an option. We no more want to think that "that's it" for them, than we want to believe "that's it" for ourselves when we pass from this world.

As a student of the Bible and a disciple of the Lord Jesus Christ, I know better than to trust secular wisdom and understanding. Where these other capable books and authors stop, I went on. Where natural understanding ends, I sought the supernatural. I could have authored yet another book on healing the human heart, but I preferred rather to find spiritual help to soothe both heart and spirit, to find real and lasting comfort to help in this time of need.

INTRODUCTION

I am going to ask you to do something that most people think is quite easy to do, when in fact, it often proves to be quite difficult. I am going to ask you to be honest with yourself for a moment. It may prove harder than you think, but no hedging. No one is privy to your inner thoughts, so be open and honest with yourself.

No matter what your spiritual beliefs or religious affiliation (or you may not even have or want one), if you are reading this book because you have lost a beloved pet friend, you are dealing with the nagging questions that haunts most of us at these most awful times, namely "Is that all there is? Will I ever see him/her again? Is there really a God who cares"?

Even our children have these questions. They are braver than we are, however. They are not afraid to ask out loud. Because of our own uncertainty, we respond with a cursory "Spot went to doggy heaven", but we know that we really are not sure. We have no basis for what we tell our children except we know that is what they need to hear. I went through this questioning period myself. I think we all do. We have these questions, but are afraid to ask them, because apparently, no one has had the answers to them, until now.

It is at that point in our grieving that the psychologist can no longer help and must take flight. It is here that their wise counsel and books can no longer guide. It is here that someone with genuine knowledge of the spiritual must rise to assist. It is for that reason and that reason alone that this book was prepared.

INTRODUCTION

If you are anything like me, you do not want closure. You want comfort and hope and answers you can depend upon. You want to know with certainty what has become of your best friend. I know of only one place to find supernatural comfort and hope that is dependable, timely and credible...the blessed Word of God.

That is exactly where this writer went to find true peace in my hour of need. My need was met, abundantly and totally, as God opened up my understanding of things I had not seen in his word before.

I think it is expedient for you to understand that I did not enter into this research as a novice. In fact, I have been a student of the Bible for more than 28 years with many years of accredited Bible courses and more than 20,000 hours of personal study in the 66 books that comprise the Old and New Testaments. Moreover, I have taught adult Sunday School and Bible studies for over 20 years. It is important to my credibility that you know that I am very well acquainted with acceptable Bible research principles and appropriate exegesis of text.

Despite my education and experience, I feel I need to offer a disclaimer. It seems that no matter how many years one may study, no matter how familiar one may become with the Bible, there is always something new and great to learn from this blessed book. Periodically, circumstances too complex or overwhelming for us to handle come into our lives that remind us just how small we are and how little we know. It is then that we discover the very deep things of God in his word.

INTRODUCTION

I may have read over a passage a hundred times before, but never saw the gem of knowledge it contained on another subject Often I find that providential guidance does not come until the time I actually need it. I find it is as if "someone" was watching and knew. We will not visit in this study the question of whether that is by coincidence or design, but if you have been there, you could never subscribe to the former.

Such was the case with my studies for this work. I had a desperate need for comfort and when I sought help and consolation from God's wonderful book, despite the fact that I had read the verses so many times before, a whole new understanding about animals was opened to me. In other words, previous to my need, I had never seen, nor considered what scripture had to say about animals. It simply never occurred to me to consider what became of them when they passed.

Motivated by need, I thoroughly researched the subject and now have full assurance of what the Bible teaches about them. I now know that God has made provision for them and that I shall see them again. I may not get to feel their cold noses at the pearly gates as the title suggests, but there is no doubt in my mind that they will be there and that a grand reunion is only hampered by the passing of time.

When one of my closest pets passed unexpectedly, it hit my wife and me very, very hard. Our children are grown and on their own and our pets have become like children to us. To lose one to age is upsetting enough. As hard as that is to accept, you are somewhat readied for the eventuality because you know that age eventually takes us all.

INTRODUCTION

To lose one prematurely however, as was the case with our Chihuahua "Pebbles", is absolutely devastating. What's more, to live with the knowledge that it didn't have to happen at all is almost completely insurmountable.

Pebbles was a beautiful dog of seven years with tan and fawn colors. We had not been able to have her spayed as the rest of our animals had been for several years. With special tests, the Veterinarian ascertained that she could be successfully spayed at age 7 with virtually no risk to her health.

I was very apprehensive about the procedure because of her age and weight (she was not obese, but very well padded at 13 pounds - we had given her the nickname of "Garganchihuahua"). But the doctor assured us it was a simple procedure and that she was now medically able to endure it.

His attempt to comfort us by saying "The operation went perfectly. She should have been okay", did little to alleviate the crushing pain we felt when he phoned with the unexpected bad news that she had passed. His comments a few minutes later when we arrived on the scene that "this had never happened before" also did little to comfort us.

Needless to say, my wife and I have punished ourselves over and over again for opting for the surgery. She really did not need to have it, but to eliminate the possibility of other health problems, it seemed the safest thing to do. It was more of a safeguard for her then a convenience for us. How we wish we had the opportunity to rethink that decision. How I wish I had listened to the little voice of apprehension inside of me.

INTRODUCTION

You do not have to go through something like this (and I hope you never do) to understand what we were going through. A terrible void of loss and guilt prevailed in our home for the next several months. For weeks all my wife and I could do was drag ourselves to work, make it through the day, and then come home and just lay in bed weeping and comforting each other.

I wrote a lot of poetry and sulky prayers. The words just seemed to pour out of my heart. I think it is human nature to do such things when our hearts are broken. Somehow writing things down helps us to feel better. At one point I even thought to write a book on what it was like to endure a broken heart, but it was too hurtful to do so. It pleases me to author a more optimistic and uplifting book like this instead.

I wish I could accept full credit for coming up with the idea to research this subject. It would be quite an ego booster to know I was that spontaneous and creative. Unfortunately, my need, not my creativity, should get the spotlight. The truth is, some credit belongs to someone else altogether. Oddly, the catalyst for motivating me was the lack of compassion of someone I counted as a friend.

One evening at church, shortly after losing Pebbles, she asked "Why are you looking so glum Gary"? I recounted the tragedy for her with tears in my eyes and a lump in my throat. Without so much as a sympathetic twinkle in her eye, she coldly, almost laughingly responded with "Oh and I suppose you think that she went to doggy heaven, don't you"? The implication was clear. She did not think so.

INTRODUCTION

That curt, unfeeling reply cut me deeply. I hadn't expected it. It was like stepping into the path of an oncoming car that I didn't see coming. Her rudeness only served to deepen my sorrow and make me feel even more alone and helpless than I already felt. I don't know how I mustered the wherewithal to not strike back at her verbally, but somehow I did. I even managed a sickening chuckle to brush the conversation away, as most of us do in these uncomfortable situations.

I confess that I was tempted to lash back at her for her insensitivity. I just did not feel like hurting her back and I was in no mood for conflict. Besides, there was an up side to this awful encounter. She unintentionally had made me face the question that I was hiding in my heart, the question I had been afraid to face. The same question many of you are hiding.

Now, there it was. It was out in the open. It had been uttered out loud. Where indeed did I think my precious Pebbles was? What was my position on this? Many people hold me as their mentor in the Bible...and I simply did not have an answer. I just didn't know. But I felt more than inept and insecure, I felt challenged. I wanted to know. And I was going to find out.

And find out I did! The Bible is full of guidance on this topic. And since I feel so certain that others want to know too, I decided to record my research and pass it along. You will have to weigh my thoughts according to your own faith and convictions, but I hope you find the comfort and hope that I found.

CHAPTER 1

FACT, FAITH AND FINDINGS

There is so much knowledge available in this world today. Students without access to a computer during the school day are quickly becoming the exceptions. They now have the world at their fingertips, and while they may not possess any more common sense than other generations did at their age, they certainly have absorbed more information and mastered the tools of our technological world.

I am told that computers, or at least certain computer groups, hold an estimated twenty to thirty pages of data on every person in the civilized world. Network news sources have estimated that the World Wide Web grows by more than 170,000 web pages every day, or over a million each week. That is amazing. At that rate, if 1,000 people read one web page every 10 minutes, non-stop, 24 hours a day, 7 days a week, for the rest of their lives, they would lose ground and never catch up. Whew!

Technology is racing ahead of us at a blinding clip. Super computers can process billions of transactions in mere seconds. It boggles one's imagination. I admit it is becoming too much for me. As I sit in front of my multi-functional, multi-colored, multi-media, voice-command computer, I am in complete awe of technology. I get headaches wondering how they get the programs on the tiny chips to work. I wonder how anyone could learn so much or be so intelligent so as to enable them to put a computer together.

CHAPTER 1

FACT, FAITH AND FINDINGS

I also wonder what the future holds. My generation mockingly laughed at the 1960's Zaeger and Evans song "In the Year 2525", when it suggested that machines would be doing everything for us and that our arms and legs would hang at our side with nothing to do. Of course, there were no PC's back then, so it was just a song. Now, I wonder. I can open programs on my PC with voice commands. I don't have to touch a key. Someday soon we will be able to operate everything we do on the machine simply by talking to it. And to think that 30 years ago the calculator was the discovery of the ages!

There are so many places we may go to in order to gather information...the library, periodicals, files and of course, computers. We can form opinions on virtually any subject, including technical subjects that are completely unfamiliar to us. We do not have to be experts, because the expert is now on the video or in the box on an electronic circuit board. We can acquaint ourselves with literally any aspect of any subject and become immediate novices through this blitz of information now available to us.

If we want to become experts however, we must leave off from general knowledge writings and refer to the technical manual. General knowledge is usually some fact mingled with a lot of opinion. That is not a condemnation, just an observation. If we want to construct a boat, we need to follow technical blueprints that give us facts. If we want to build a gas turbine, that too requires technical expertise and facts that can only be obtained from the accepted technical manuals.

FACT, FAITH AND FINDINGS

So too, this topic of life after death after life. There are literally tons of non-technical reference materials out there on this subject, written by all sorts of people with all types of credentials, and motives. They give you some fact and a lot of opinion. They are not technical, but qualify rather as general, basic knowledge. If we want expert fact and guidance on this topic, we must go to the technical manual. The technical manual on life and death is, in my opinion, the Holy Bible. In this matter of animal afterlife, use of the Bible becomes so much more important because there is a lack of general knowledge available to help form an opinion.

It is here, in the Bible, where we learn of mankind's (meaning men and women from the Greek word Cosmos) beginning, end, and eternity. Many may scoff at the Bible, but that does not alter the fact that this book alone has an authority unknown to the sum total of all other books written by men and women, including this very one that you are reading.

Nevertheless, many have put that self-proclaiming truth aside and undertaken, with nothing but their own opinion as a basis, to produce writings that are in conflict with the Bible. This does not diminish the unimpeachable authority of the Bible, nor detract from the account of mankind it contains.

I do not wish to offend anyone with my position on the Bible. I merely wish to establish from the outset, that I revere the Bible above any other writing and that the Bible is the technical manual that I consulted and yielded to in all of the conclusions I draw. Where better could someone turn to learn about the hereafter, than to the timeless, yet timely book that was authored by the one who lives there?

CHAPTER 1

FACT, FAITH AND FINDINGS

I think a quote from this great book will underscore why I rely on the Bible so totally for comfort and guidance. I know the quote is taken a bit out of the context for which it was given, but the tenet of comforting others that it sets forth is prevalent throughout scripture. Simply, it reads:

"Wherefore, comfort one another with these words".

I Thessalonians 4:18

These words were penned by the Apostle Paul and delivered to the church at Thessalonica. They were intended to be thoughts of encouragement and comfort, not only for them in that time, but for any and all who would place their trust in God the Son. His words teach us a valuable principle that I would like to address. To do so, we must first understand the circumstances that prompted his being directed to write to this church. This may take us on a short rabbit trail, but I assure you, it is important to the case I am building.

The faith of the Thessalonians was wavering. They were making the classic spiritual mistake that most believers make at one time or another in their Christian experience...they were "thinking" instead of "believing". Faith is the "substance of things hoped for, the evidence of things not seen" (Hebrews 11:1) - or, in other words, faith is believing God. Doubt was starting to take hold. They were wondering what had become of their departed loved ones. Paul assured them through these inspired passages that they would meet their dead in Christ again. What a marvelous comfort this must have been to them. To have such a giant in the faith confirm the promise of God to them.

CHAPTER 1
FACT, FAITH AND FINDINGS

Now, before you raise a wary doctrinal eyebrow, let me assure you that I am not trying to include animals in the event that is addressed in this portion of scripture, an event endearingly known to those of the Christian faith as the "rapture". I am rather, illustrating the attribute of God to exercise providential care over the grieving and to give them comfort and hope as he did here through the Apostle Paul. His word is full of examples of his caring and loving nature. The principle is clear...we are to "comfort one another" in spiritual matters. It is in obedience to this command that I offer my thoughts and conclusions on the many issues associated with what happens when our wonderful pets come to the end of their earthly road.

If you are taking time to read this book, it is likely that you are doing so because you have recently had the misfortune of losing a pet, or perhaps are concerned that you someday will have to face that eventuality. Since our life spans are so much longer than that of the animals we take as pets, unless you are very old and yourself at risk of expiring, the chances very good that your concerns are justified.

A very dear friend of mine by the name of Will, one of the most kind-hearted people I have ever met, asked me rhetorically one morning in regards to his three year old dog named Sweetheart, "Gary, what will I ever do if she dies"? Will and his wife had no children. They were wrapped up totally in their little girl Sweetheart. I know Will loved her deeply, like a child, because she was spoiled just like someone spoils a child. He once brought her to my office and put her on the floor to introduce her to me. She promptly squatted and soiled my carpet. All Will could manage through his ear to ear grin was "Isn't she precious"!

CHAPTER 1

FACT, FAITH AND FINDINGS

Then Will asked me a question that he obviously wanted an answer to. He said "Gary, do pets go to heaven"? Will knew that I was a Baptist preacher and knew the Bible well. I knew he was expecting an answer, and I wish that I could have given him one, but the truth was, I just did not know.

The question therefore, went unanswered. Now, a dozen years later, as I bring my work and research to paper, Will and Sweetheart come to mind. If Sweetheart is still alive, she would be nearly 16. I know Will is still alive and well for I have kept tabs on him and once a year or so we exchange cards or e-mail. So one of the first copies of this book off press, will be heading to my good friend. I am happy that I will finally have been able to answer his question. I know he will rejoice to know that he will see his Sweetheart again.

If you are anything like Will or me, then I suspect your motive for reading this book is to find answers, to find comfort for the loss you feel. If that is so, coincidentally, your reason for reading this book parallels my motive for writing it. I simply was seeking comfort for the pain of losing a very special and very close friend.

One could misconstrue the contents of this book then as nothing more than wishful thinking, and that I was grasping for anything to bring my grieving heart relief. While I have no doubt that my grief moved me to seek answers and help from the scriptures, I assure you that I was dreadfully aware of the danger of allowing my heart to make the Bible say what I wanted it to say and I guarded myself diligently from being so swayed.

CHAPTER 1
FACT, FAITH AND FINDINGS

My grief did not cause me to abandon the fundamental principles of research. I know all too well how one can fool themselves into applying what they want to be true to what is actually true and I did not want to fall into that trap. I do not mean that people are intentionally deceitful, but rather that they allow emotions to sway them into massaging what is said into what they want to hear.

I assure you that I did not build and document a self-serving case. I will admit that had my research led me to conclude that animals would not have a part in the afterlife, I probably would not have written a book on the subject. It would have been too depressing to do so. Nevertheless, if the Bible did teach that, I would have accepted it as truth, and somehow managed to cope with that awful revelation. Thank God that this was not the case and it is clear that he loves these creatures and finds great pleasure in them.

Actually, while grief served as the ignition to get me started in my research, it did not remain my motivator for long. Somewhere early on in my research, during prayer and meditation, my grief took a back seat to enthusiasm. I simply love the Bible, and I love learning new things from it. I began seeing things about animals that I had never seen before. It absolutely staggered me that I had spent so much time in the Bible and never paid any attention to this subject.

As a result of this discovery, I have spent thousands of hours studying and learning and have come up with many exciting conclusions and ideas that I want to share with you. I have tried to capture each of my observations as clearly and honestly as possible.

CHAPTER 1

FACT, FAITH AND FINDINGS

I must confess that there is not an abundance of scripture that addresses the eternity of animals, which may explain the total absence of books on the subject throughout the ages. Still, God gives us a wealth of passages associated with animals and how important they are. We are able to build upon the principles taught in these associated scriptures in order to draw some very solid conclusions. I will cover most of these in the sequel to this book, but we will visit enough of them here to meet our purposes.

While the exact topic of animal afterlife is not specifically addressed in detail, I want you to understand that there are many other subjects not addressed directly in the Bible, for which we humans lack no opinion. We take stands on all sorts of things, often claiming we are taking a Biblical stand, when in fact, there is no specific guidance.

How do we arrive at these spiritual positions we take? Simply, we use the tools God has provided to each of us. We look at applicable passages, evaluate other, related principles found in other passages, consider all the associated non-Biblical information and apply deductive reasoning (logic).

Let me give an example of how these tools work together to give us discernment on a particular subject. Consider the subject of illegal drugs. Is there anyone in the civilized world today who is not enlightened about the ill effects of natural or synthetic chemicals upon the human body? I should think not. Even those who are enslaved by these habit-forming drugs and who continue to punish their bodies day after day with them readily admit that they wish they could free themselves from the suffering it causes them.

CHAPTER 1
FACT, FAITH AND FINDINGS

Now then, the Bible mentions drugs in several places, none which really could be applied to prove overwhelmingly that drugs are harmful. The Bible does not say "Thou shalt not use cocaine", for instance. We have no clear teaching on that particular drug. We know it hurts our bodies. We know it is illegal to possess and use. But hey, the Bible doesn't specifically mention cocaine, so....

We are told to "rightly divide the truth" by the Bible. In other words, we are to let it interpret itself. By comparing scripture to scripture, we can arrive at constants or truths. To conclude cocaine is okay by the Bible is to wrongfully divide the word of truth. If we know it is harmful and sometimes fatal to our bodies, we know the Bible teaches an associated principle that precludes the use of cocaine. The Bible teaches we should care for our bodies as a temple. Applying logic tells us not only that cocaine is not good, but that it is in fact, bad.

There is no clear guidance, but building upon principles from the word and applying logic, we arrive at a conclusion, a very solid one at that. Similarly, when it comes to our beloved pets, there is no clear guidance that says "animals go to heaven". However, we can use the same tools we used in our example to arrive at a supportable position on this topic.

Obviously I cannot assure you that all the conclusions in this book are iron clad, right on the mark, exactly as I tell you facts. I believe them to be, but I am only a man. I labored hard to arrive at the conclusions I offer. I would not mislead, nor would I ever present something as fact if I were not convinced it were so.

But, to be fair, this is new ground we are covering. To my knowledge, no one has ever attempted to research, catalog and expound upon this topic from a Biblical perspective before. I received virtually no help in my research and spent many long, tiring hours on this project. Consequently, the potential for error in some of my "ideas" exists. Someone, perhaps you, may come along and say "Hey, good job, but did you consider this"! I welcome your constructive input. You might enhance this work and have a hand in helping someone in need. That is how technical works are refined.

Having said all that, the bottom line for me is that I feel very confident that the conclusions I present in this book are factual and a close representation of the way things are. Embodied in my confidence however, beyond the research, is my faith in God and his good will toward his creation. That faith was a critical factor in my research and therefore, contributed greatly to the development of my conclusions. As a consequence, while I know my conclusions to be true and am able to transfer that knowledge to you, I cannot transfer my faith. That is something you will have to provide.

I will promise you however, that if you read this entire book and evaluate my work honestly, when you have finished, you will come away with some new things to think about. Most of all, I hope your heart will have found a comfort you had previously lacked.

CHAPTER 2
CREATURE OR CREATION

SECTION A - THEIR BIG DAY

There are any number of views of how, when and where animals originated. Some are religious or faith based. Others are not. Largely, they are all in contrast with each other. It is not my intention to agitate anyone, but I do need to discuss the most popular views on this topic, as my position will serve as one of the foundational footers for this chapter, and perhaps the entire book. I realize that people in all the major camps of thinking are equally passionate about their views. If your view is somewhat in contrast with mine, I hope you can understand how my passion drives me to hold the convictions that I do.

The three most popular views are evolution, theistic evolution (more currently referred to as "Superior Design") and creation. There certainly are others, but in our western culture, these are the top three. I will give a brief overview of each in the following pages.

Predictably, I sit in the camp of creationism. I am a Christian and my faith hinges on the authority of the Bible. If I am to believe at all, I must believe it all. How anyone can believe part of the Bible and disbelieve another part is beyond my comprehension. If we were wise enough to discern what is inerrant and what is not, we would have no need for the Bible at all (for the record, I believe it all to be). That notwithstanding, the Bible teaches that animals were created and I accept that. If you do not share all of my convictions concerning creation, that is fine. Please continue reading. The goal of this book is to comfort you, not to convert you to my way of thinking.

11

CHAPTER 2
CREATURE OR CREATION

On the other hand, if you totally reject creationism and/or the Bible or God, I must honestly advise you that you will most certainly not enjoy this book. Belief in God and scripture is foundational to many of the concepts and conclusions I discuss. I do not wish to mislead anyone. This is why I ensured the title clearly suggested that the book was Christian in persuasion (i.e. "Pearly Gates").

I feel compelled to point out before I define each of the three teachings, that if I were writing this book 200 years ago, this chapter would not be necessary. This is because 200 years ago there would have only been one position to discuss...creationism. The other two major philosophies are virtual newcomers, whose origins (forgive the pun on evolution) are somewhat presumptuous and untrustworthy, to say the least.

Now then, let us move on to the overview of the three major views of how life, and therefore, animals began. I will list them in reverse popularity order. This is not my opinion, but the statistical result of conducted polls.

First up, but least popular view: **EVOLUTION**.

I have read much of Darwin's work, and the works of several of his successors, or rather, supporters. I consider these men and women to be sincere in their beliefs, but I do not consider them to be correct. Many of the proponents of evolution expect their assumptions to be accepted by the general public without the scientific validation and ratification that they claim the Christian faith lacks.

CHAPTER 2
CREATURE OR CREATION

Faith neither claims nor needs scientific validation; although there is overwhelming scientific evidence to support the claims of the Bible. For true Christians, faith is the evidence of things not seen. It is taking God at his word and believing him, and requires no physical proof.

Despite the inability of so called "science" to validate the claims of evolution, that is not my primary problem with this view. What bothers me most about evolutionary evidence is that it hinges more on faith than faith does. Let me explain. If you have read any of the dissertations that generate from this group of people, especially from papa Darwin himself, you cannot help but notice that there is a commonality present and prevalent in their writings. In everything I have read, assertions of fact are almost uniformly preceded by qualifiers such as "perhaps", "could be", "I think" or "maybe". Evolution, from my perspective, requires a whole lot more faith than does faith itself. And if I am going to put faith in a person, it is going to be the infinite person of the Lord and not a finite person much like myself.

The evolutionist basically excludes God from the equation altogether, and credits the persevering adaptability of the creature and nature's ability to select the strong and eliminate the weak as the reason for life and its progress in evolution. Evolutionists may say they still believe in God, but in the final analysis, they must deny him in order to embrace their doctrine. If they come close to recognizing God at all, it would be in their attempt to personify mother nature or mother earth by giving credit to that perceived deity for all that happens in our world.

CHAPTER 2
CREATURE OR CREATION

As tempting as it is to me to refute the assumptions of evolution, this is really not the time or place to do so. I have already said more than I had intended. To say more would serve no purpose other than to dominate the available time and space and further irritate those who do not share my views on evolution. It is sufficient to say that evolution not only eliminates God from the whole picture, but in so doing, precludes the existence of an afterlife for either man or beast...in other words, no need for God then, no need for God now, no need for God later.

Up next: **Theistic Evolution**. As I previously pointed out, this close kin of evolution is a relatively new position on the origin of life, one that has drawn much attention. It has lured away many from what were considered evolution and creation strongholds. It is difficult to say whether this view has overtaken evolution theory in popularity, but if it hasn't, it no doubt soon will. It is safe to say however, that it has won converts from both evolution and creation circles.

Let me be as simple in defining this view as I possibly can be, so we do not confuse the two lines of thought. Theistic, from the root word "theo", or "of or pertaining to God", when put together with the philosophy of evolution, suggests a blending of evolution and creation doctrine. In other words, God had a hand in provoking the evolutionary progress of the planet and all the species that it is populated by. Proponents of this position contend that we can now accept the doctrinal claims of evolution because they do not infringe upon the teachings of the Bible about creation. Conversely, evolutionists can accept God and the account of creation because there is a viable meeting of the two teachings.

CHAPTER 2
CREATURE OR CREATION

Here is how they manage this...they say that the "day" mentioned in the Bible is not a literal 24-hour period. Instead, they assign an arbitrary number of years to each of the six days of creation, such as 1,000,000. In other words, each day in the Bible really represents 1 million years. I said the number was arbitrary, because some scientists do not subscribe to the 1 million year assignment, but chose rather 1 billion years.

It is interesting to note that they can be so sure that God did not mean what he said, but they cannot even agree among themselves as to the measure of time. Regardless, the intent is obvious. They want to make evolution more acceptable to those who cannot stomach a straight shot of evolution. It is a compromised position to neutralize and win over opponents to evolution theory. And it has worked quite well.

Besides finding this philosophy objectionable and unsupportable, I find this obvious ploy to "sneak" in the evolution idea under the cloak of theism in keeping with any misguided attempt to make the Bible support one's personal view.

Even the most cursory or elementary study of the Bible would show each day of creation to be a literal 24-hour period. The scripture clearly states "the evening and the morning" were the first day. The same words are used in many different places in both the Old and New Testaments, each time alluding to a 24-hour period. Are we to interpret the Lord's request to his disciples to "watch until morning" to mean he wanted them to wait around for a million years? Of course not. But that is what we must believe if we change the measure of time assigned to the word "day".

CHAPTER 2
CREATURE OR CREATION

I do not expect supporters of the Theistic Evolution view to accept this explanation. To do so, they would be inclined to also acknowledge the authority of God's word over their own supposition. That is a very hard thing to do. It is much easier to correct what they see as an obvious error by God in the creation account.

I had not intended to refute anything about evolution, but I just must offer this one scientific argument for your consideration. I assure you that there are many other strong arguments, but this one is one of the hardest to ignore. If we look at Theistic Evolution with a purely scientific eye and apply literally the claim that is made by evolution, to wit: that each day represents a designated period of time (let's say 1 million years); and acknowledge that during this time natural selection and development of the existing species took place, then we run into a very big scientific problem.

Applying other accepted rules of science, such as photosynthesis for example, we cannot reconcile the long periods of time assigned to each of the six creation days. In other words, if we have plants being formed on one day (or over a period of 1 million years), animals during a subsequent million years and the sun appearing after that, how did the species survive at all?

We know by scientific principles that plants cannot survive very long without sunlight. But according to some Theistic Evolutionists, they survived a million years without sunlight. Even more outrageous, a billion years according to others. It is simply amazing that these plants flourished in the dark for such a long period of time. But then, who can argue with science?

CHAPTER 2
CREATURE OR CREATION

Oh we are not done yet! We still must reconcile the problematic theory that plants and animals existed so long without the mutual exchange of oxygen and carbon dioxide they supply to each other. Science tells us that neither can live without the other for any extended period of time. But again, Theistic Evolutionists would have us believe they did just that for millions, perhaps billions of years.

Just think about that period of time...millions, perhaps billions of years. That is an extraordinary long time to go without critical elements needed to sustain your life. Think how very impossible that would be. Think of how long it takes to live our lives. What would our earth be like without the sun during your short lifetime? Take away the plants and the animals too. It just would not work. You could not possibly survive. And we only live for about 70 years or so. Now imagine 13,000 generations of your descendants living under those conditions and surviving. And I only used 1 million years as our base. Most evolution "authorities" speak in terms of billions of years. Whew! Talk about needing faith to support what you believe!

The impact of such a drawn out ecosystem would be quickly felt and life would die off as rapidly as it appeared. Plants could not live without the sun. Animals could not live without the plants. I am not saying that the entire chain of life would break down. I am saying it would never be established. Life could not exist under this imagined matrix.

Theistic Evolution then, is a hard pill to swallow, more difficult even than the theory of evolution itself. Not only does it include most of the preposterous assumptions of evolution, but it becomes unscientific and self-defeating in its own doctrine.

CHAPTER 2
CREATURE OR CREATION

Finally: **Creation**: Some time back, perhaps 20 years ago, I recall reading some of Darwin's writings. I was not really curious about evolution, but I could hardly discuss or refute his views if I had never acquainted myself with them. As a Bible student, I immediately detected a difference in Darwin's writing from the estimated forty men used to write the books of the Bible. It was not convincing. It was even less than that. It was weak. His case was weak and the evidence he presented was questionable at best.

I could not put my finger on why there was such an overwhelming perception of insecurity in his writing. At first I thought it might just be his style of writing, but it was not. Then I discovered that it wasn't the author or the subject he wrote on that disagreed with me. It wasn't even the amazing jumps that were made to arrive at some of the conclusions he drew. What really bothered me was the utter lack of conviction and certainty with which he presented his so-called "evidence".

After so many years, I am sure that I could not quote any portion of his work accurately, but I vividly recall an avalanche of disclaimers that he used throughout his work. I remember counting several hundred times the use of the words and phrases "maybe", "perhaps", "I think" and "it could be". I admit, I do not know what was in this man's mind or heart, but as a writer I can affirm that a book usually projects the writer's thoughts and ideas. With this in mind, his use of such non-persuasive language suggests a lack of conviction. I have a hard time understanding how the philosophical descendents of Darwin can be so strong in their beliefs when Darwin himself appears not to have been.

CHAPTER 2
CREATURE OR CREATION

Conversely, the account of creation is relayed to us via the best selling and therefore, most popular book in history. It is housed in a book that has been used to successfully prove historical and archeological fact, facts that scientists and historians often disputed, without basis or success. For instance, in the book of Daniel we are told that Nebuchadnezzar was once the king of Babylon. Historians balked at this account for many years. They assured us that not only had this man not been the king, he had never even been to the city of Babylon. Imagine their surprise when twentieth century archeologists uncovered the ruins of Babylon and found that not only had Nebuchadnezzar been to Babylon, not only had he been the king of Babylon, but that every brick in the city had his name imprinted upon it.

Which is more palatable to the human heart and spirit: a book written by a finite man, which seems to lack conviction; or an infinite book written by an infinite God that has authoritatively found its way into the homes of countless masses? Without even addressing the supernatural uniqueness of the Bible, we must recognize its immeasurable worth in history, geography, culture and social reform. Moreover, it is a book of unmatched authority and wisdom, with no instance, not even one hint of supposition or guess work. Rather, it overwhelms its reader with certainty and authority and instills strong faith.

Creationists are so called because we accept a literal rendering of the creation account of Genesis Chapter 2, to wit: plants on the third day, sun, moon and stars on the fourth, birds and fish on the fifth and all other animals and mankind on the sixth, all days being a literal 24-hour period of time. They all survived because they did not have to exist long alone, but almost immediately found themselves in a mutually supportive role.

CHAPTER 2
CREATURE OR CREATION

Having removed any doubt as to my position on animal origin, let us move on to a discussion of the actual day of the creation of animals, their big day if you will. On day five, the fish and birds arrived. We will put them aside temporarily and address them collectively with all other animals later on. I prefer now to move on to day six, the day when the animals that science calls "mammals" were created.

SECTION B - THEIR PURPOSE

It is at this point that we need to make a distinction as to what animals we are primarily concerned with in this matter of afterlife. Let me say first, and as clearly as I can, that I feel certain that God has a plan and place for all the creatures he has created. Chapter 4 addresses this subject in greater depth. The singular thrust of this book however, is to give comfort to those who have lost animals that they love. I understand that this opens up a very wide range of animals. It could include wild animals that we have befriended, domestic beasts of burden or farm animals that we grew up with, but in my mind, we are primarily speaking of those animals that come from that group of wonderful creatures we have come to call "pets".

From this point forward therefore, I will use the term "pets" and "animals" almost interchangeably, but my thoughts will lean more toward domesticated animals, especially those we allow to live among us in and around our homes. In no way does that exclude the others, but let us concern ourselves with those who capture our hearts and share our lives.

CHAPTER 2
CREATURE OR CREATION

I think it is important to note that wild or undomesticated animals did not always exist. In fact, domesticated beasts of burden did not always exist either. There were no wild animals in the beginning. There were no plow horses or working oxen. All animals were tame, given the role of companion to mankind, and both dwelled together in peace and harmony.

In fact, the harmony was so profound, that God tasked Adam with naming each animal at his discretion. I think we have all wondered where Adam came up with some of the names he assigned. Whatever gave him the idea for aardvark or platypus? Why ostrich or orangutan? No doubt, the closeness that animals and humans enjoyed allowed Adam an insight we no longer enjoy today. It is difficult to second-guess him now.

In light of all this, it is not a stretch of either truth or imagination to assume that all animals originally existed in a "pet" status. It is convincingly apparent that this was precisely the role God had intended for them to play. We can safely conclude then, that God (and please if you get nothing else from this book, be sure to grasp these key points):

- knew what he wanted to do in regards to creation
- had the power to bring his plan to pass
- created a perfect environment
- created man in a perfect state of spirit, mind and body
- created perfect animals to share perfect mankind's perfect domain
- intended for this perfect situation to continue forever, without death for either human or animal

CHAPTER 2

CREATURE OR CREATION

When he had completed his act of creation, we are told that God surveyed his perfect work and gave us this assessment of what he had made:

> **"And God saw everything that he had made, and behold, it was very good"**

> **Genesis 1:31a**

He was very, very happy with his work and with the relationship he had orchestrated between mankind and animals. Lest we forget who we are talking about here, it was GOD who did the work and GOD who made the assessment. We aren't talking about "the man upstairs" or "the big guy", irreverent terms I have come to detest. We are talking about GOD, who alone has power to create and take life. He created, and he created perfectly. And he was very pleased with what he had created.

The fact that this perfect situation would eventually change is not because God created us with a flaw, but rather because we exercised our free will to bring imperfection into our lives. As a result of man's tragic fall away from God through disobedience (discussed in greater detail in Section 2:c), our animal friend were also changed and we now have wild beasts and beasts of burden.

Animals now fear man. I cannot say that I blame them after what we did to their perfect world. Still, our relationship with them was not totally lost. From the ruins of our original relationship came a group of animals we simply refer to now as "pets".

CHAPTER 2

CREATURE OR CREATION

Another result of the fall of mankind manifested itself in the plant world. Previously, man and animal consumed fruits, grains and vegetables. Neither man nor beast labored as they co-existed in peaceful harmony, eating the abundant fruit and vegetation. Food was plentiful. Now, after the fall, it did not grow as plentiful as before. Now people were forced to till the ground and toil to obtain it.

Man now hunted for and consumed meat to offset the diminished vegetation. He had to work to survive. His load was heavy. He learned to depend upon domesticated beasts to help him do his work. He fed the beasts in return. The harmonious co-existence was now more of a co-dependence. To this day, even though our pets still serve in the role of companion, they also are, to varying degrees, beasts of burden, serving as K9 police, sled dogs, mousers on farms, etc. Some even breed or show their pets to supplement their incomes.

Despite that, the lion's share (I couldn't resist using an animal cliché) of pets are loved and cherished as companion animals. In truth, the relationship is still one of mutual dependency. They give us love and devotion. They greet us after work and make us feel special. We in turn give back love and provision and make them feel special. It is an age-old relationship, dating back further than anyone can remember or research. As long as there have been people and animals, there has been a relationship between them. And what a grand relationship it has been, transcending every ethnic and cultural border, in every climate or topographical setting, at sea, in space, on the frozen tundra or in the dry desert, in peace or war, throughout every age, pets have been by our side as an intricate part of our world and history.

CHAPTER 2
CREATURE OR CREATION

You can find their images painted on the walls of caves, captured in medieval sculpture, and immortalized on canvas. Presidents have brought them fame. Cities have erected statues of them. In a thousand ways, as long as mankind has existed, we have paid tribute to these wonderful creatures which have walked at our side.

Their unreserved loyalty and dedication has generated a wealth of written testimonials. For those of you who have computers, I urge you to search any number of websites under the keyword "Pet Loss". On one hand these places are sad to visit, perhaps one of the saddest on earth, because literally thousands of goodbye notes and stories about pets are posted there. However, there is also an air of honor and nobleness present as we read of champions and fathom the impact they had upon the lives of their humans. I spend a lot of time reading these accounts. I could never post my own as I am just not that strong. I keep my pain private. This book is a major step for me, sharing a very personal part of my life with others.

There is no doubt but that these wonderful furry and feathered best friends are an intricate part of who we are and what we are about. I recall many years ago, one of the most endearing testimonials to this that I have ever come across. While on active duty in the U. S. Coast Guard, stationed at home in Hawaii, an electronic message (not e-mail, but a radio transmitted signal) came across the wire. The message was for all Coasties in the entire district, which basically included all of the south Pacific. It seems Shackles, the mascot dog on one of our Loran stations on a tiny atoll, had passed away of old age.

CHAPTER 2
CREATURE OR CREATION

Hundreds, if not thousands of sailors had stroked that dog's fur over the years. Shackles had provided companionship to many lonely souls stationed at that isolated outpost, so many miles from home. Many a sailor had found him a faithful substitute for family and friends. He lifted their spirits and made home seem a little closer for them.

When he passed, the hearts of those who were currently stationed with him were broken and they felt compelled to send a message out to other sailors in the Pacific basin who may have known this fine friend.

To understand the significance of this act, you need to know that this sort of message is strictly taboo over official military communication nets. Infractions are not tolerated and disciplinary action is usually swift and sure. Despite the rules, not one complaint was registered by any of the thousands of user installations. In fact, the message was received and passed on from command to command until almost every unit in the Coast Guard had received word. If you didn't know Shackles, you knew of him. He was a sailor. He was a shipmate. He served his country well until he could serve no more. And then he was given a sailor's farewell.

Our history, our culture, is peppered with accounts of great animals and the great help and service they have been to us. Their tales touch us deeply and dearly. I know there are a million stories, but I think sharing a few of the ones I am familiar with would be an appropriate way to honor them collectively. It might also serve to cheer up the grieving and maybe soften the hearts of those readers not yet convinced of the eternal importance of these wonderful creatures.

CHAPTER 2
CREATURE OR CREATION

I will not cheapen my attempt to magnify our animal friends by alluding to stories of Lassie, Rin Tin Tin or Morris the cat. While these were all intelligent and entertaining characters, they were nothing more than actors in our living rooms and the stories they played out the concoctions of Hollywood writers. I have no doubt but that each of them were great pets to someone, but they were just animal thespians to the rest of us, champions of the make believe. I chose rather to recount a few stories about real life, touching episodes of almost unbelievable determination, achievement and dedication...to show that animals have had and continue to have important roles in this world and the next.

Almost immediately, one story comes to mind that was in a Honolulu newspaper more than two decades ago. It seems an Australian rancher was taking a break from the hot sun. He had walked to a nice little bluff overhanging a lake and had stripped down to his unmentionables to take a dip. As he made his way to the edge of the bluff, intending to dive in, his herding dog jumped in front of him and began to growl.

The rancher was startled. The dog had never acted like this before. He was a kind-hearted dog who got along with all the other animals and people on the farm. It was so unlike him to display such a mean temper. He shouted at the dog "get out of the way dawg", and started again to the edge of the bluff. The dog again blocked his path, this time showing his teeth and growling even more viciously than the first time. The rancher, wondering if his dog had gone mad, again scolded the dog, saying "what is wrong with you dawg, get on out of the way", while making a sweeping motion with his foot.

CHAPTER 2
CREATURE OR CREATION

Apparently seeing that he was not going to stop his master from going to the bluff, the dog turned and ran off the edge of the bluff himself, falling the 5 or 6 feet to the water below. Almost immediately the water exploded with a large splash and the dog let out a blood-curdling cry.

It took the rancher only a moment to realize that the dog had been grabbed by a large crocodile that had been sunning itself below the bluff. The dog, with its keen sense of smell, was immediately aware of the presence of the crocodile and sensed danger. The dog had done the only thing he knew to do to keep his master from entering the water. He blocked his path and growled a warning. That failing, in total devotion to the person he loved, the dog sacrificed himself. What courage and devotion!

Do not despair. There is a happy ending to this story, at least for the dog and rancher. In barely a moment the rancher realized what was happening and quickly retrieved his revolver from its holster on the fencepost where he had hung it. He jumped into the water and dispatched the crocodile in time to save his best friend's life. The dog was torn a bit for the worse, but made a full recovery.

Stories of dogs and extraordinary events are more prevalent it seems than say cats, horses and other common pets. This is understandable I suppose, because dogs are used in many service-oriented areas, such as K9 patrols, drug detection, ski patrols, and the like. Searching and finding seems to be a tailor-made role for canines, rather than for other animals. So stories of their accomplishments are going to be more numerous.

CHAPTER 2
CREATURE OR CREATION

Take for instance, the recent rescue of a lost toddler in the northeast in sub-freezing temperatures. It seems no one could find the lad, despite an intensive search. Searchers began fearing that the cold would beat them to the child, so they called for more searchers. It did not help. Darkness fell and the search was called off until morning.

In desperation, they released the family dog into the night in hopes it might achieve what the rescuers could not. As the dog disappeared into the night, no one actually believed it would do any good, but they were grasping at straws as the temperature dropped.

In the morning, searchers were up at first light. They found intermittent dog tracks and searched in the general direction the tracks seemed to lead. Expediency and determination seemed to have waned as all hope for finding the child alive disappeared with the setting sun the day before. Searchers moved almost lethargically through the brush and snow.

Several hours later, one of the searchers let out a loud triumphant scream, "we found him, we found him alive". Excitement spread through the ranks of the searchers as rumors came down that the boy had been found alive. And indeed he had been. Half exposed, half pinned beneath the large family dog, the smiling face of the toddler peeked out at the first rescuer on scene. The dog had not only located the boy, but had taken the matter under control by holding him down and providing warmth throughout the freezing night. The first searcher said it seemed the dog knew they would be coming and was holding the lad until they did.

CHAPTER 2
CREATURE OR CREATION

Extraordinary stories may be dominated by dogs, but they are certainly not limited to that species. How many times have we read of the cat that warned the family of fire, carbon monoxide or other danger? How do they do these things? I can only suppose that they are driven by love and devotion. What other explanation will work?

I know that I made a distinction between wild animals and pets earlier, and my intention was to exclude the former to focus on the animals we interface with on a daily basis. However, sharing the above stories of courage and perseverance has brought to mind several other accounts of helpful animals that have impressed me throughout the years. Please indulge me while I just briefly give credit to some of our non-pet friends of the animal kingdom. It will help solidify my contention that animals still retain a sense of companionship with us humans. I will explore this thought further in Chapter 5.

Certainly you recall the very recent situation where a toddler fell into a gorilla enclosure and was knocked unconscious by the fall? To the amazement of all the horrified onlookers, the biggest beast in the pen moved over to the child, tenderly lifting him into her lap and cuddled him until help arrived. During the wait, she also fended off the attempts of some younger gorillas to play with the unconscious child. When the zookeepers came, she readily gave the child over to them. This was not an isolated incident. About a decade earlier, a similar situation had developed with basically the same result.

CHAPTER 2

CREATURE OR CREATION

At least a few of you will recall the story of the woman from the Philippines who had found herself adrift in the Pacific Ocean after a boating mishap. Far from shore with no flotation device and virtually no hope of survival, she clung to life as long as she could. According to her personal account, when she was sure that she could tread water no longer, resigned that this was how her life was going to end, a large sea turtle surfaced within arm's reach. She grabbed hold of the turtle's shell and held on.

She managed to climb up partially on the back of the massive turtle. The animal did not seem to mind at all. Miraculously, the turtle remained with her throughout the reminder of the day, through the evening and night hours and well into the next morning. She even managed to sleep for a few moments.

As light flooded the ocean the next morning, there was a ship on the horizon, a cruise ship it would later turn out, with hundreds of people (and therefore witnesses) onboard. Unbelievably, the turtle began swimming in the direction of the ship. When turtle and ship met, the turtle began circling the ship, as if looking for a place to deposit his cargo. When a platform was lowered near the turtle, the turtle sounded (submerged), dislodging the woman, and it was not seen again. Many people witnessed this great event.

It is kind of spooky, isn't it? But when you consider the countless stories of porpoise saving swimmers and factor in the myriad accounts of animals providing services to people in so many ways, surely you can see that the original bond between ourselves and animals still exists on some level, even in the wild.

CHAPTER 2

CREATURE OR CREATION

This relationship between animals and people not only benefits us. There are many instances where people have gone to bat for animals, often at great risk to themselves. One particular story in the Topeka, Kansas Capital Journal in January of 1997 really moved me, causing me to think more seriously about this bond we have with animals. Just listen to this. I swear it is true...I was in town when it happened. I'll give you a brief version of the story that appeared in the newspaper on that day.

A local farmer had two horses. Actually, he probably had more, but the story was about these two particular horses, Shammy and Guyan. These two horses were siblings and lifelong companions to each other and the farmer for more than 24 years.

Shammy had fallen through the ice on the farmer's pond in sub-zero wind chill weather and was not able to climb out. He had fallen into a part of the pond that was over his head and it was all he could do to stand on his hind legs and get a breath. In fact, he was able only to poke part of his snout through the ice-clogged hole he had made in the ice with his fall. Even his eyes were under water. The farmer had no idea that this had happened, but knew something was dreadfully wrong when Guyan came running up to the house, stomping and whinnying frantically. She was carrying on in a way that let him know something had happened to Shammy.

The farmer followed Guyan back down to the pond, assessed the situation, ran back to the house to call the fire department, and returned quickly to the pond to help hold Shammy's head above water. The fire department arrived and a successful rescue was mounted.

31

CREATURE OR CREATION

Later, when speaking with reporters, and much relieved that the incident had not resulted in tragedy, the farmer was quoted to have said "I don't know what I would do if I had lost him, they are just like children to us". To quote another famous (although fictional) character associated with the great state of Kansas "ain't it the truth, ain't it the truth".

And this case is not unique, but rather typical of the allegiance people feel toward animals. I am not talking about animal right activists and the like, although they certainly care about animals. I am speaking rather of just everyday, common folk like you and me. How many times in the past few years have we picked up a newspaper or switched on the television to see hundreds of people giving their all to save groups of beached whales or porpoises? As I watched the people work feverishly to save them, my heart was in my throat and I wished I could have been a part of their effort. And what of the sea otters and turtles that the communities in California and the Florida Keys have spent tens of thousands of dollars on to repair missing flippers or broken bones? And what of the granddaddy of all acts of good will toward animals...the rescue of the two whales caught miles from the ocean in Alaska several years back?

How well I remember that episode. I followed it more closely than I did the Gulf War. The picture of those two whales trapped and facing certain death as their air hole slowly froze over; and the hundreds of people rushing to their rescue will stay with me forever. As the people worked to cut holes in the ice for the whales to breathe, then moved a few dozen yards forward to cut other holes, while other people encouraged the whales to swim to them.

CHAPTER 2

CREATURE OR CREATION

The progression moved forward hour after long hour, until the entire landscape looked like the perforated line on a form. The whales eventually and gratefully swam out into the open water and I believe the entire nation rejoiced.

Though people and whales could not communicate, the people knew what was needed of them and the whales seemed to understand what was expected of them as well. The many holes cut from love have long since frozen over again, but the picture of that day lives on in the memories of many and is a memorial to the good will of people toward animals and representative of the link we have with the animal world.

The people in these stories were driven by more than love of animals. Something deep inside tells us that we have a connection to the animals, not that we evolved from them, but that we were created with them. Certainly it is conceded that people benefit greatly from the companionship of animals. Studies have shown that people who share their lives with a pet generally live longer. Programs today are placing pets with the residents of retirement homes because there is strong evidence that animals fill the emptiness and loneliness experienced by the elderly and lift their spirits. Quality and longevity of life is positively impacted where animals are part of the care.

But the door swings both ways in this relationship. Billions of dollars are spent on and for our pets each year. We pamper them and love them, clip them, comb them and clean and powder them. We spend fortunes ensuring their good health. We have Veterinarians, animal hospitals, specialists and even animal psychologists. When we cannot afford or have not the place to keep them, some of us adopt and sponsor them.

CHAPTER 2
CREATURE OR CREATION

We sing songs about them, write books about them, compose poetry and immortalize them in so many ways. There are no less than three major cable networks that run animal programs virtually 24 hours a day (that is the literal Bible day, not the evolutionist's). There are dog shows and cat shows and horse shows and rabbit shows and pet expos and well, I think you get the idea.

We have a national network of helping hands like the Humane Society, SPCA and several other organizations who strive hard and do their best to rescue as many animals as they possibly can. Then, there is the World Wide Web, where literally thousands of sites and hundreds of thousands of pages are dedicated to our wonderful animal friends. It is certainly a mutual relationship, one that both sides benefit from and enjoy.

In light of all the above, and considering the evidence that follows, surely we can see that God has an eternal plan for our animals. I explore this subject much more deeply in the sequel to this book, so I won't go into detail here. Allow me to just say that God is not a God of the temporary. He does not make things on a temporary basis. I have already explained how this applies to the creatures he has made, but it applies also to the relationship he has forged between man and animal.

There is no doggy heaven, no kitty heaven. Similarly, there is no people heaven. There is God's heaven, that place where he dwells. He has made room for us and the angels. Surely you can see that he has made room for the other creatures he has made. Considering that he hung a billion planets on nothing, making room for all of us should prove to be no challenge for him.

CHAPTER 2

CREATURE OR CREATION

The question will undoubtedly be raised "but where would he possibly fit all the animals that ever lived"? Well, for that matter, where would he fit all the people that ever lived? These are valid questions. Unfortunately, I cannot give you an exact answer because there is no scripture that speaks directly to this question. I am willing to speculate a little though. Interestingly enough, during one of my many visits to the dentist years ago, I happened upon an article dealing with over-population. The article was written by someone with a whole lot more smarts than I on this topic. The author applied some mathematical equations to the known world population and came up with a unique and sobering conclusion. At least, it was sobering to me.

He concluded that the world wasn't as over-populated as we might think. He justified that comment by saying that if it were possible to accomplish the task, there would be enough land surface in the state of Texas to accommodate a single family house for every living person (not family mind you, but person) on earth. That is an amazing claim. Nevertheless, if you have been through that great state as many times as I have, you will have no trouble accepting his findings. It might be a bit crowded, but it sure looks like it could be done.

Now then, if you can mentally form a picture of Texas in your mind....got it? It is a large chunk of real estate is it not? Now, surround Texas with the rest of the United States mainland in that picture, and all of a sudden Texas isn't all that big. Now add the remainder of North America. Then add South and Central America. Now the other continents of the world, including the 11 time-zoned Soviet Union and the immense continent of Africa. Texas seems to be quite small now.

CHAPTER 2
CREATURE OR CREATION

Finally, take the sum of all that, which is our entire planet, mix it into our solar system and then the entire universe that we are aware of, which consists of billions of stars and planets, some thousands of times larger than our own, and I think that it is very easy to see that God has more than enough room just in the physical realm we are aware of, to house all of his living creatures.

CHAPTER 3
COMMUNICATING

SECTION A - TALKING

Although unique and perhaps even revolutionary, I believe that the evidence presented thus far is an accurate representation of available fact. I put much effort and all of my heart into this work, spending long hours researching, praying and meditating. I read everything on this subject that was available, and believe me, it was not much. Most of it was dated and hard to relate to today, such as C. S. Lewis's dissertation about animals and their souls.

I even queried the Library of Congress for similar manuscript information, but the kind ladies who searched for me could not find any copyrighted work. Consequently, my major source of information was the Bible. That may cause some to scrutinize my work with a bit more skepticism, but I welcome that scrutiny. I wish more people would check out what some say in public more closely, rather than accepting at face value what they say. Our world would be a better place if everyone knew certain facts firsthand, rather than knowing them the way someone wants them to know them. I am sure that in my case, you will find that I have not embellished on any of the facts set forth in scripture.

That said, let me state with equal emphasis that what follows in this chapter is without doubt speculation on my part. I have little basis for my conclusions other than that it makes sense to me based upon the research I have conducted. I have no definite scriptural basis for what I address in this chapter, but there are some scriptural "hints", for lack of a better description.

CHAPTER 3
COMMUNICATING

There certainly is nothing that is in contrast with, or refutes my speculation, but that is not enough to prove that I am right in this matter. I will leave it up to you to decide if my ideas have merit or not. At the very least, I hope I make you think about the possibilities I present.

Previously I told you that we will see our pets again. That is factual, as far as I am concerned. My work has been challenged by several fellow ministers, including the Chancellor of a major Christian University. They had never studied this out for themselves, but somehow still considered my ideas preposterous. When I laid out the facts offered by scripture, many changed their way of thinking, but some did not. But they could no longer argue with it either. Honest people cannot change scripture. Rather, they are changed by it.

What would you think if I told you that not only do I know that we will see our pets again, but it is possible that we may be able to converse with them as well? I can hear some of you now as you think "and how hard did you hit your head"?

Admittedly, it is a bit off the beaten path of conventional thought, perhaps even a bit bizarre. But please allow me the opportunity to explore the possibility with you, and allow yourself the chance to hear a new point of view. If you close your mind to a thought, please do so only after hearing it out and weighing any existing evidence. Often, the best lessons come from unconventional thoughts and actions. Long before the airplane ever flew, the concept of human flight was mocked and those who thought such thoughts considered possessed. Yet today, flight is routine. Millions of people fly each day.

We lock ourselves in with tradition and routine. I am not condemning either. I am merely suggesting that without creative thinking, new doors never open. Sometimes we open new doors and must shut them up again, and that is okay. But I think most of us want the chance of knowing what is on the other side before we permanently close it. So please accept this idea as it is intended, a speculation, a possibility. If you are still with me, you might as well continue on. It isn't going to hurt you and you might just enjoy what I have to say.

While I am quick to point out that this is speculation, that does not necessarily mean that I do not believe it to be a very real possibility. In fact, I do believe that animals can communicate. There are some very interesting things to consider. And that may be all they turn out to be....interesting. If that is the case, what have we lost by considering them? We have lost nothing but a few moments of our time.

But what if I am right? What if animals can talk? What an amazing eventuality that would be! Could you imagine the conversation you might carry on with the cat that you haven't seen in 30 years?

Now, before you echo the initial reaction of some of my colleagues and dismiss this idea as preposterous, please remember that previous to this point I used persuasive, factual approaches for every point I made. I was careful not to hazard a guess, unless I told you first that I was doing so. I have not changed my approach. I will not abandon logic or reasoning. I have already advised you that this section contains much speculation on my part. However, I also maintain that it could, and probably is, true.

Consider what I have to say and draw your own conclusions. I cannot make you agree with me. If I could, I wouldn't, for this is simply my opinion. But it is an opinion based upon evidences that are hard to dismiss. These thought-provoking evidences follow in no particular order.

Thought 1...

Let's start in the beginning. I mean the beginning of time. Let's go back to that brief innocent period of time we call the Garden of Eden. The devil, the Bible tells us, assumed the form of a serpent and spoke to Eve, tempting her to do something she was not supposed to do.

Eve responded to the serpent. In fact, a short conversation took place. I am not going to recount the conversation, for that really is not important to this section. Everyone has heard the story anyway. Instead, I want to point out that the most amazing thing about their conversation was that they had one at all.

How would you react if you were in your garden and you came across a snake and it spoke to you? I am sure it would shake you up a little. Snakes aren't supposed to talk! Anyone would react with great alarm if an animal of any kind began a conversation with them. There is no indication however, that Eve was at all taken back by the serpent having the ability to speak. She didn't hesitate or wince in any way. Instead, she responded to him as if it were a normal occurrence, or as if it had happened many times before.

CHAPTER 3

COMMUNICATING

Eve was not shocked. She did not react as if it was something that should shock her. She did not react like you and I would react. The only logical conclusion is to think it was not an unexpected thing, but one that was normal in their innocent world. Without a doubt, I believe both Adam and Eve had talked to this serpent before. On that I am not speculating. I do wonder though, if the rest of the animals in the garden did not have the same ability of speech.

Thought 2...

Many birds have the ability to speak...parrots, parakeets, ravens, crows, myna birds, and others. Some might contend that their speech capability is limited, and perhaps that is true. But I have seen some birds with almost insatiable appetites for learning new words.

A good friend of mine had a place of business where he allowed his personal parrots to roam freely during business hours. One particular bird, an African Gray by the name of Lola, was a remarkable bird. She could almost carry on a conversation with a person, and she had this talent of being able to duplicate sounds. She could emit sounds like a truck backing warning signal, the television alert test signal and a host of other sounds.

Her particular forte was imitating the ring of the telephone. We kept a portable phone in the shop and when it rang it was always a major undertaking to find it because we were all in the habit of leaving it wherever we finished our last conversation.

CHAPTER 3
COMMUNICATING

We received a lot of telephone calls during the day and invariably, when it rung, everyone would sort of just freeze and look around at everyone else who was obviously trying to remember where the phone was last left. Chaos took over as everyone raced around looking under this or that for it.

Apparently Lola enjoyed hearing the telephone ring. It seemed to break up the humdrum of the day for her by causing an exciting flurry of activity. So she took it upon herself to master the ring. No one encouraged her to do it. She just decided to do it on her own.

I do not know how long it took her to duplicate the sound, but I remember clearly the day she chose to unveil this new talent to us. We were sitting around doing little one day, when the phone rang. As usual, we jumped up, gave that stunned deer in the headlight look, and scrambled around looking for the portable. My friend found it first, clicked it on and said "hello". Then he threw the phone down and said "I hate it when people hang up". No sooner had he thrown the telephone down, then it started ringing again. He picked it up again and said "hello" and threw it down again, this time cursing.

A few minutes later, it rang again and he made me pick it up. Again, there was nothing but a dial tone. But this time I had noticed that the phone and its base were to my left, but the ring had come from my right. It didn't take us long to figure out that the noise came from Lola. We decided to put the telephone down again and this time we watched her. Sure enough, it was her. She was busted!

CHAPTER 3

COMMUNICATING

We thought being discovered would make her stop, but we were in for a surprise. She performed this little "trick" for us several dozen more times over the next couple of weeks. Each time the telephone rang we would look at her and she would look so innocent, that we answered the phone. Many times there was no one there and that innocent look quickly turned into a devious "gotcha" look.

We put our heads together this time and decided that no one would answer the phone on the first ring anymore. Oh, this bird was dealing with a brain trust now. True to the plan, when the phone rang, we waited for the second ring before answering it. As a side note, now that we were involved in this game with Lola, the telephone was never misplaced again. We kept it right in plain sight as we were eager to show that bird who she was fooling with. So with each second ring, whoever answered the telephone, would, saying "hello", cover the speaker apparatus, turn to Lola and say "not today stupid", just to rub it in.

Imagine our surprise when just a day or two later, the telephone rang, we waited, rang a second time, we answered, and found we had been suckered again. She had learned and adapted. She had apparently understood and accepted our challenge. She learned to ring twice, and even three times, with perfect intervals in-between the rings. But here is the kicker and the part that lends to my communication theory...this time when she grinned at us with that devious "gotcha" grin, she added the words "hello stupid". Now, you may say she was just mimicking the words we said to her, but she wasn't. She took one of the words and added it to another to consciously and purposely mock us. At least, that is the way it looked to me, and I was there.

CHAPTER 3
COMMUNICATING

Fortunately for us, she tired of the telephone game and moved on to other tricks, like disappearing out into the parking lot. She would wait for someone to come in the shop, slip through the door while the hydraulic closer eased the door shut. She did not fly, she walked everywhere. And she was not trying to escape. She had the life of a queen. She just liked walking out the door and coming back in later.

Apparently bored with just walking outside, she would go out and stand on top of someone's tire on their vehicle (under the fender well) and yell out loudly "where's Lola" until someone found her. What a personality that bird had.

Then, returning to evidence of animal communication, there was the time I was showering in my home in Hawaii many years ago. I was just scrubbing away and almost at that point where one breaks out in song, when from out of nowhere came this unfamiliar voice saying "good morning". Completely surprised, I tried covering myself with my hands thinking someone was in the bathroom with me...and someone I did not know at that.

I looked out of the shower stall and there was no one there. I couldn't imagine where the voice was coming from because I was alone in the bathroom and it was on the second floor. Then they said it again, "good morning". I looked in the direction of where the voice had come from and my eyes came to rest on the two screened panel windows above the shower (temperatures in Hawaii rarely go low enough to require closing the windows, and installed screens allow steam to escape).

CHAPTER 3

COMMUNICATING

I squinted to look through the screen and there on the pinnacle of some sort of protrusion on the roof, was a Myna Bird, a bird with a painted grin on its face that makes it look like it is always smiling. If you have ever been to Hawaii, you could not possibly forget that grin or the goofy hop hop hop step they make (a lot like the Heckle and Jeckle magpie cartoon characters).

I looked at him and he said it again, "good morning", and gave me one of those head-twisting looks. I returned his "good morning" and he hopped closer to the screen window. He actually looked like he was going to start a conversation. Instead, he simply repeated his salutation, twisted his head a few more times, and then flew off, presumably to peep at someone else in the shower.

It was an interesting encounter. For a few moments I wondered to myself if the bird actually knew what he was saying, but I really didn't care about such things in those days, so my mind quickly wondered in another direction. Today, reflecting back, I wonder about birds and this ability they have to speak. Is it just an ability to mimic the sounds they hear, or is it a leftover attribute from an earlier ability to communicate intelligently?

Thought 3...

Animals communicate with each other. This is a fact we must acknowledge. We see it happen before our eyes almost on a daily basis...dogs barking, birds chirping, cats meowing and so on. Science has documented many forms of communication between animals. Some of the methods they employ are more complicated than others, but all are effective means of communication.

Commonly, this communication comes in the form of an audible sound, but sometimes it is silent (at least to the human ear). Some creatures use a whistling sound or a series of clicks, grunts or growls. Others, like dolphins and bats, send out high frequency sound waves that are interpreted by others with the appropriate receiving apparatus.

Whatever means are used, there is no denying that animals communicate with each other, and that they do so effectively. Other animals know exactly what is being said to them. It is not outrageous then, for me to say that animals "talk". Talking is simply a form of communication, the relaying of your thoughts to another. The thoughts do not have to assume the form of words that you and I understand to qualify as "talking", they merely have to be understood by the receiver.

The truth be known, animals are sometimes more effective communicators than humans. Now, I did not say, nor do I mean that they are more intelligent or have a vocabulary equal to ours. I merely said they are more effective at times. That is because, unlike humans, animals always communicate what they mean. There is no pretense with their "speech" as there is with human communication.

Often, we humans will say something that could have more than one meaning. For instance, a curious fellow employee might ask innocently "Gee I wonder how Molly got that job"? She was just expressing curiosity. Another employee, motivated by jealousy might respond more suggestively, "Yeah, I wonder what she did to get that job"! We witness innuendos like this all the time. In fact, we are probably guilty of them ourselves.

Not so animals. They are straight-shooters. How many of you have ever been deceived by your cat? She purred after you stroked her, but you know she didn't really enjoy it. She was putting you on to stay on your good side. Of course she enjoyed it...cats cannot help but purr in pleasure or wag their tails when irritated. It is their nature.

How many of you have come home to a lying dog? Well, I suppose I ought to rephrase that question. I am sure many of us come home to find the dog lying on the floor, or the couch or the easy chair. What I meant was, how many of you have ever come home to find a dog that tried to lie to you? I mean he was in a real bad mood. His day was awful. He had several accidents on the carpet, went for his annual rabies shot and even had to endure yet another bowl of dry dog food!

He didn't feel like running to the door to great you. He didn't want to have to put on that dumb happy face act again like he has so many other times. His tail was sore from the shot and he just couldn't possibly wag it right now. But he knew that was what you were expecting, so he came running to the door, jumping and wagging that tail for you. He even beat it against the wall a few times, "thump, thump, thump" because he knows that makes you laugh. And then when you bent down to pat him on the head, he slobbered all over you, wagging that sore tail "ouch, ouch, ouch". What a big fibber!!!!

Obviously these are not serious questions or situations. Animals simply do not lie. Now sometimes they might bluff, as in the case of a mother protecting her young and growling. She may even fake a charge at a perceived threat to her offspring when someone gets too close. But actually, they aren't really bluffing, but rather giving a warning. And that warning is real. There is no pretense to it. Take the warning or suffer the consequence is the message being sent. When animals communicate, they mean what they say. We could learn a lesson from them. What a better world this would be if everyone learned to speak honestly.

Even insects communicate. Some of their societal networking is so intricate and so much more efficient than ours, one wonders how anyone could believe that we humans are so much more "evolved". For goodness sake, a simple termite colony runs better than the largest city ever built, minus the crime and poverty.

But I am wandering off track again. The point I wanted to make under this thought is that animals communicate. They speak in many ways, by color and appearance, by posture or gesture and audibly and inaudibly. They speak to each other and they speak across species lines. They also speak to humans. We may not always understand them, but often we do.

My little Westie had a difficult time learning that she wasn't supposed to piddle in the house. Eventually the light went on and she said "oh, that is what you have been trying to tell me". She then learned how to tell me it was time to perform that function so that I would open the door and let her outside. The longer she waited to tell me, the more excited her communication would become. If I listened to what she was saying, everything went well. But when I didn't listen, well, it was time for the paper towels. And this story leads me to my next thought.

Thought 4...

Pets communicate with their people. In fact, most, if not all animals that are associated with people communicate, or try to communicate with people. For example: dolphins and whales have a discernable language. They use their language very effectively. Large groups of them travel and live together in great harmony because they can speak to one another. Hunter groups work together to herd schools of fish, matriarchs protect offspring by telling them where to swim in the pod, and we could enumerate many other examples if needed. We have managed to decode and document their language. We have even managed to duplicate the sounds they use in order to speak back to these creatures in a language they understand.

Admittedly, their language isn't very complicated, but it is effective and it works for them. It works for us as well. We replicate the sound-words and they respond to their trainers in the desired way. We have also elevated their communicative abilities by teaching them part of our language via sight and sound signals.

Our household pets have proven to be equal, if not superior to, our ocean mammal friends. They learn quickly to communicate their thoughts to us. As I pen these words, my terrier is doing a little dance in front of me with her pull toy dangling from her mouth. I have no doubt what she is trying to communicate to me. She has several dances that she performs, each with a different meaning. There is no mistaking the meaning of the dance she is doing at the moment, because of the prop she has in her mouth. Did I say prop? Perhaps I should have said prompt. Either way, she is delivering her message very effectively.

I now am faced with three possible choices, one of which I must communicate back to her. I can stop what I am doing and reach for her toy, which will make her very happy, but take me from my work. I can tell her "no, not now" and her ears will drop along with her toy and she will walk off with a very sad countenance. In fact, she will over-emphasize the sadness. They can be such actors. Finally, the choice I opt for...I can simply continue typing, which she will eventually interpret as "not now, maybe later". She will then either curl up at my feet and wait or she will start playing by herself. Whatever option I take, we have both effectively communicated to each other.

We all know that this type of interchange is not limited to dogs. Many, if not all animals have this capacity, especially those that are domesticated. I once had a kitten that made the same demands upon me as the dog I mentioned above. Her toy was a string with a small piece of cloth wadded up and tied to one end. She loved to paw this wad of cloth. I kept her toy on top of my dresser in the bedroom. If I went in the bedroom for any reason, she would jump up on my dresser, snatch her toy, jump down on the bed and bother me until I gave in and played. She did not meow once, but she communicated her thoughts to me quite adequately.

No doubt you remember the television commercials where they show a dog or cat apparently talking. Some are obviously staged and the videos doctored. Others are merely common pets that make uncommon or unusual sounds. One local roofing company asked the dog in their advertisement "what are we best at fixing", and the dog of course responded "roof", or something close enough to it to make you think it did.

CHAPTER 3

COMMUNICATING

The idea was simple and effective. People love animals and they enjoy humor...so when you combine the two, it is bound to be a hit. I have no idea if it actually increases sales for these companies, but it certainly does cause us to remember their company's name and what they do. Does that translate into our thinking of them when the time comes for us to use their services? It has not for me, but I suspect for some it does.

Another video used on one of those home video programs spoofed a cat that was being given a bath in a tub. The cry of the cat was captured on the video as it struggled to get away from the person washing it and out of the tub. The cry was an unmistakably drawn out "nooooooooooooooo". I realize that the cat was not actually saying the word. Rather it was uttering an irritated version of its "meow". Or was it?

Am I suggesting that animals can say words? Of course certain animals can say words. Take the myna bird I spoke of before. The real question is "Do they consciously pick the words they say because they know what they mean"? I honestly do not know. One could make a convincing argument either way. Let me share one made by a very dear friend of mine.

He had a very intelligent Cairn Terrier who he swears used words all the time. For instance, when the dog wanted to go outside to take care of business, it would sit in front of one of the family members and say "out". They swear that the dog used the word in the same way they used it when training her as a puppy. The word uttered by the dog was a bit more drawn out, so that it sounded more like "ooooouuuuuuu". Obviously the dog had trouble forming the "t", but my friend swore the tone and emphasis resembled the word they had always used.

Of course, to be cordial, I gave him a cursory "uh huh" and let it go at that. A talking dog indeed! I was not convinced. Imagine my surprise when visiting in my friend's home many years later, the dog sat in front of us and said "oooouuuu". There was no doubt in my mind that the dog was speaking to us. It was quite amazing. I half expected the dog to say "thank you" when it came back into the house.

Since that time, I have encountered many people with dogs, cats, and other pets, who assure me that their pets genuinely try to communicate with them. I mean the animals actually are trying to form words. I have had many, many pets, but have never been as fortunate as some of these folks. All my pets prefer their own "tongue" to that of humans. None have been bilingual. Nevertheless, their ability to communicate their thoughts and emotions to me has not been diminished. By using sounds, body language and gestures, they have adequately communicated to me.

Thought 5...

There are numerous references to animals in heaven in the Bible. That is well known by anyone who regularly spends time in this book. Little attention is paid to the "other" creatures mentioned in the book of the Revelation and some Old Testament books.

These creatures appear to be a form of animal as much as anything else. In fact, my speculation is that they are a cross between animal and angelic being, but I can offer no proof for that opinion, only my own impression. I explore this opinion and offer more evidences in the sequel to this book, which is in the works, therefore we will not discuss it here at length.

CHAPTER 3

COMMUNICATING

Now, the word "animal" does not appear anywhere in scripture. Instead, the word(s) "beast", "creature", "creeping things", "everything that has breath", etc. are used. Therefore, speculating that these "other creatures" are related to animals, in part or whole, is not a great stretch. Certainly they are not human.

What type of animal they are is not important. What is important to our study is that they speak. They use audible, understood words in worship of God the Father. More importantly, it appears this is not an uncommon or unique occurrence in scripture. A serpent spoke to Adam and Eve, a donkey spoke to a prophet, and these creatures in The Apostle John's presence.

Now, let me switch gears here and couple this thought with a principle that you might think abstract, but that I think applies. Doesn't the prayer we commonly refer to as the Lord's Prayer say "thy will be done on earth as it is in heaven"?

I readily acknowledge that these passages have nothing to do with animals. However, the principle implied is that Heaven (and therefore the things that are normal there) is the way God wanted things to work on earth. He made the Garden of Eden a perfect place. There was no illness, no sorrow, and no death...just like in Heaven. In Heaven, creatures speak. In Heaven it is not unusual for them to do so. It is reasonable to believe then that the same was true on the earth in the beginning. Just because things have changed on earth because of the rebellion of God's prize creation, is no reason to think that the creatures of earth did not have the ability to speak as do their counterparts in Heaven.

CHAPTER 3

COMMUNICATING

Thought 6...

Revelation Chapter 5, verse 13 says...

"And every creature which is in heaven, and on the earth, and under the earth, and such as are in the sea, and all that are in them, *heard I saying*, Blessing, and honor and glory, and power, be unto him that sitteth upon the throne and unto the Lamb for ever and ever".

There is so very much to discuss about this verse, most of which I will withhold for later on in this book. It is important to note here however, that portion of the verse that I placed in italics. The Apostle John, who authored this book under the direction of God, said "heard I saying". In other words, he heard the creatures (animals) speak. I realize that this word is inclusive of humans as well, but if you will study all the elements of this verse out, you can only conclude that it is speaking of ALL creatures created by God.

Now, remember that this is a prophetic book about future things and this has not yet come to pass, but will one day. Nevertheless, it is a very solid piece of evidence that animals have the ability to speak. The evidence "speaks" for itself.

Conclusion...

Are any of these thoughts overwhelmingly convincing as to the ability of animals to speak? No. Independently, each thought is comprised of some fact and some speculation. Taken by itself, with the exception of thought number six, each thought is a weak argument.

Collectively, however, they give us considerable cause to believe that animals have the ability to speak, or at least once did. These thoughts mesh together to give us a preponderance of the evidence, which is the staple criteria in our legal system of proof. The evidence is not undeniable, but it is very convincing. Far less evidence has been accepted to establish religious dogma on more important issues.

Acceptance of this idea boils down to the open-mindedness of the individual weighing the evidence. Human nature is a peculiar thing in regards to what we believe. Once a person has adopted their set of beliefs on a particular issue, it is very difficult to convince them otherwise, regardless of mounting evidence for an opposing view. If therefore, you are not yet convinced, I hope at least you have come to the point where this idea is less radical to you than it was when you began this chapter. I will leave off from making case on this issue for now, but will pick it up again in chapter 5.

SECTION B - BODY LANGUAGE

I find it very difficult to deal with the memories of departed pets, even though I am certain that I will one day see them again. I have never handled separations well. Bidding a temporary farewell to our pets is similar to leaving the people you love when you must travel. You know you will be reunited in a few days or weeks, but it is difficult to be separated from those you are accustomed to being with.

As a young man during the Viet Nam era, I found myself stationed aboard the USS FORRESTAL (CVA 59), an attack aircraft carrier stationed in Norfolk, Virginia at the time. As a new husband and young father, it was difficult to endure the long six or seven month deployments away from home. I made two and a half such cruises and several lesser-length deployments in between, which were required to keep the crew and equipment prepared and seaworthy. We all knew we had an important job to do for our country by keeping a vigil in strategic waters, but that did little to lessen the loneliness one feels when away from family and friends. Despite the fact that there were over 5,000 other men onboard, you couldn't help but feel alone sometimes.

It was always great to head home. I remember the ship showed movies on the close-circuit network onboard for 72 solid hours while making the 3 day transit from the Azores to Norfolk. They knew most everyone could not sleep, so they provided entertainment to keep us occupied. We were zombies when we arrived home, but such was the life of a sailor. Those of you who have been deployed while serving in a nautical service know what a thrill it is to dock at homeport and see thousands of loved ones cheering your ship in.

56

CHAPTER 3
COMMUNICATING

Remembering and missing loved ones who have passed is much like being away on a trip. You know you will see them again, and you count the days until that great reunion. The same is true of the pets we have lost. They are family to us and we miss them dearly. The difference is that the separation is usually a lot longer than that of a deployment and you must deal with the memories and the waiting for a lifetime. And memories can be very difficult to handle at times

I am one of those sentimental types. Some would call me a hopeless romantic, but I have never understood why being romantic made one hopeless. Indeed, romantics are very hopeful people. That notwithstanding, I am the type of person who drops tears during any number of touching movies or the playing of the national anthem (as long as the singer is reverent). In fact, the truth be known, I suppose that I am hyper-sensitive.

I do not mean to portray myself as some wimpy kind of guy. In fact, just the opposite is true. I have a reputation for being very athletic. I used to fight as a black belt in Shodokan Karate and won many tournaments. I have caught and tagged alligators for Everglades National Park in Florida and generally am a pretty tough guy. Still, when it comes to moving life happenstances and movies, I suppose I am a wimp. I cry when Olympians persevere over hardships and injuries, regardless of what country they represent or whether they win or lose. I go numb when the news reports another child missing. I cried when Dumbo was separated from his mother, when Old Yeller died and when Demi Moore saw Patrick Swayze at the end of the movie "Ghost". Now, as a student of the Bible and follower of the Lord, I do not endorse the theology of that movie, but I can't help but be moved by the romance of it. After all, I am a hopeless romantic!

Sad as my condition may sound, I do not believe it is fatal. Besides, I have always enjoyed being this way. While it is embarrassing to try to inconspicuously wipe away tears during a moving movie in front of company, my emotions validate to me that I am a caring and responsive person. I do not thrive on pain or look forward to sorrow, but somehow emotional pain makes me aware that I am alive and that there are more important issues in this world than some of the things we concern ourselves with.

The downside of being sensitive of course, is that I have a harder time than most in dealing with memories. Many of you probably relate to this. Memories of pets that have passed often become a source of great pain. In no way do I mean to suggest that our memories are not endearing. Oh my goodness are they ever endearing! Still, for people like myself, they often rekindle the deep sense of loss so that it is almost as if I am enduring the initial shock of that loss all over again.

Frequently, in idle moments, I let my mind wander to special moments I shared with my pets. When these moments occur, they always provoke immediate grief. The touching recollections of their adorable personalities and unique way of communicating become so vivid and so real. I get so caught up in the memory that it almost seems they are still with me. Crashing back to reality only serves to sadden me again.

It is just for that reason that I keep my guard up against memories, allowing them in only when I know I have both the time and privacy to grieve. I am sure you know exactly what I am talking about. It hurts to remember, but it is so necessary to do so.

CHAPTER 3
COMMUNICATING

I know I rambled on a lot about sensitivity in this section. I did not do so without purpose. This section is about our pets' abilities to communicate with us through the use of body language. Sensitivity toward your pet is an absolute must if you are going to interpret what they are saying to you. I have observed insensitive people missing the boat with pets they claim they love.

Many people neglect their pets in this area of communication. They may feed and water them, walk them, take them regularly to the clinic, and do all the things necessary to provide for and protect them. But if they are not communicating with their pets, they are neglecting a very important need. Pets need to talk to us. They have emotions and ideas that they want to communicate to us. Imagine how frustrating it is when they are eager to say something, but no one is paying attention!

One cannot be sensitive in one thing and not in another. Sensitivity therefore, is a requirement for someone who truly wants to communicate with their pet. I do not mean by this that you have to be a boo hoo baby like me when it comes to romantic things, although there is nothing wrong with that. I simply mean that you need to be sensitive enough to the needs of others, human and animal, to be able to recognize certain body language. I know when my wife is sad without her ever telling me. I certainly know when she is upset with me before she ever has to spell it out. Body language and gestures are important to a good relationship and sensitivity is the instrument that allows you to perceive and interpret the signals. If you do not enjoy a communicative relationship with your pet, you need to work on your sensitivity and awareness.

Animals need us to be sensitive to their attempts to communicate. We are as important to them as they are to us. When your best friend is pawing at your leg while you are watching the news, he is trying to tell you something. When they do their little "dance" or if they just sit in front of you and stare, there is probably a message to be received. When an animal tries to communicate, the body language can take any number of forms. But when they are successful, and see that you got the message and are going to react appropriately, the body language is usually predictable. They jump for joy and act silly. It is my opinion that it isn't so much they realize they are getting what they were asking you for (i.e. water, food, a walk, etc.), but more that they are gleeful for having talked to you.

One of our current babies, who I mentioned earlier as my West Highland White Terrier named "Missy", is quite the cutie, possessing an extremely sweet nature. She brightens up our home. And is she ever smart! (I hope there is some truth to the notion that pets reflect the attributes of their people).

She is just a sweetheart...just about the perfect dog, quickly fitting into the family unit and adding so much joy and happiness to our lives. Don't laugh at me, but I sometimes take my lunch hour and rush back home the 12 miles just to throw the ball for her a couple of times. Physically, she is your typical Westie, with a pretty white coat and stout and alert countenance. She has one deformity however...a very pronounced overbite. We saw an advertisement in the paper - the breeder was going to probably put her down if someone did not rescue her, because she did not measure up to their standards. I do not mean to suggest that all breeders are of this caliber, for there are some very good ones...but there are some very bad ones too.

Back to point, her overbite has caused her no discomfort and is not a problem for us. However, she (and we) discovered that her overbite causes a very peculiar snapping or popping sound when she bites at something and misses. As a puppy she would bite at a hand or toy in play and in missing, her jaws would clamp shut on nothing but air. This would create a unique popping sound and a very humorous situation for the family.

When Missy discovered that her popping sound made us laugh and that after we laughed at her we would hug her, she quickly capitalized on this good fortune. When she wanted something or when she got herself in trouble, she would employ her popping sound, prancing around, turning her head from side to side, and snapping her jaws shut, "pop, pop, pop".

In no time she developed the noise into a sort of language, which she accentuated with body movements and gestures. She has now mastered several "acts", each employing all of the above mentioned antics, but each also distinctly different, performed for different reasons. One act means she wants food or water. Another means I want to go outside. Another means it is play time.

I know you will raise an eyebrow, but once in awhile she doesn't want anything from me but to just talk. I will be sitting at the computer, perhaps answering questions readers send to me, and in the silence of the room, she "pops off", so to speak.

She has food, water and we already played. She has her own door to go outside when she wants. There is no need being expressed, except that she wants to talk. So I will talk a little human to her, and then I will mimic her popping sound, which seems to excite her even more (I wonder what it is I said).

CHAPTER 3

COMMUNICATING

Each of the pets this family has shared their lives with have had quite unique personalities, which in turn gave them uniquely different ideas on how to communicate. Without exception, all have employed body language, sounds and gestures to communicate with us and we have been sensitive enough to have known they were doing so. Only those who have kept and loved a pet of their own and who have been sensitive to them, can truly appreciate that animals have more than an ability to communicate...they have a need. When you couple this inter-personal behavior with their wonderful personalities and devotion, it makes their companionship more desirable than some humans we have known.

It is usually for these reasons that people prefer to keep pets. They are exposed to the cute antics and body language...the almost bewitching looks animals are so famous for giving. They communicate love and devotion without ever saying the words. Before you know it, that pet has a permanent place in our heart and home.

Once in the home, the animal almost invariably bonds quickly and more closely than one could imagine. Homes are enriched by this addition and family bonds made stronger. In time, this non-human personality becomes part of the human family and learns how to communicate with other family members. It makes for a wonderful relationship and is the reason why many first time pet people become life-long pet people. If your animal does not appear to be communicating with you, I suspect they are, but you are not listening.

SECTION C - LISTENING

The process involved with mailing a very important letter is probably a good representation of how the mechanics of communicating work. Communication, in any form, cannot be considered successful unless the intended audience receives the intended message. If that important letter does not get placed in the right mailbox and delivered to the right person, the effort to communicate fails. In oral communication, the same principle applies. The message can be transmitted, but if it is not heard, it really cannot be considered successful communication.

If the pet/human relationship is to be successful, it is important that we listen to our pets. Likewise, it is fundamental that pets listen to us and understand what we are saying. Since pets depend upon us for sustenance and protection more than we rely on them for what they contribute to the relationship, it is paramount that we exercise a modicum of control over their daily activities. We do that by communicating effectively to them.

While some may balk over my use of the term "control", it is precisely that control that keeps them out of danger as they live in our world. Let me give you an example of what I mean. I was jogging one sunny afternoon in Miami, far outside the city in an area known as horse country.

As I worked my way along a very scenic road, I noticed two Weimaraners running toward me from deep inside a very large and unfenced yard on the opposite side of the street. They were coming toward me from about 200 feet away at a very quick pace.

Although they were barking and charging, they did not appear to be ferocious. It seemed they were more bent on making a point than attacking me. They wanted me to know that they were defending their master's property from all intruders, including the dreaded jogger.

I have absolutely no fear of dogs anyway. I was more concerned about their safety than I was my own. If I was on the other side of the road nearest them, it would not be a problem, but calculating their speed and determination, I knew they would not stop at the natural border of their yard. They were certainly planning to cross the street to make sure I knew they were on the job.

What they did not know was that there was a car coming down that road at a fairly good clip and it looked to me that it was going to arrive at their point of crossing just about the same time they did. There was nothing I could do to get the attention of the oncoming car's driver in time, so I did the only thing I could do. I stopped, faced the dogs and yelled loudly in a very demanding and authoritative voice, "**STOP**"!

Both dogs stopped in their tracks, almost in cartoon fashion with their legs slipping underneath them. They stopped just before reaching the asphalt road, at almost precisely the same moment the car went whizzing by. The dogs looked at each other as if to say "man, he's mean...and he is on the other side of the street after all". They then turned back toward the house and disappeared from sight, never knowing how close to tragedy they had come. I was very happy to have been of service to those animals. I am happy also that their owner had taken the time to communicate with them and teach them obedience to commands.

Animals we allow to live in our world with us are subject to dangers they usually are not aware of and listening to us is so very important. The outcome of this situation was favorable due in large part to their ability to listen and understand, which I am sure is a result of their people taking time to condition them to do so. I think about those beautiful dogs now and then and wonder if their luck is still holding. I certainly hope so.

Their story helps me illustrate my point. Animals are able to listen and understand. I am not saying that they sit around all day thinking "I hope my master tells me to roll over later", but once the request to do so is made, they remember and are able to discern what is meant. Habit or conditioning? Perhaps. However, I think it is more.

It is exactly this ability to understand and respond in the animals we adopt as our pets that cause us to accept and love them. Now, I realize that there are exceptions. Some pets do not possess that capacity, not even if we incredibly stretch the criteria.

Reptiles, amphibians and fish for instance, do not communicate with humans in the true sense of the word as we have used it in this study. Through repetition, they may know when it is time to eat and they become more active and responsive at those times. They may even recognize or actually tolerate the presence of one human over another. Their apparent excitement, and their ability to distinguish the difference in people is due to the sustenance they anticipate rather than preference of one person to another.

Do they love us? As an amateur herpetologist, with much experience in the field of reptiles and amphibians, I am compelled to say that they do not. We certainly get attached to them. We certainly grieve their passing. But we do not hold them in as high regard as a pet that can reciprocate our affections with love for us. Even the reptile which enjoys the best reputation for co-habitation with humans, the iguana, falls far short of the capacity of some of the lowliest mammals.

Take for instance, the domestic rat. To most people, the little gray, tan and white mammals are not much different from their wild cousins who scour the sewers and garbage heaps for a living. They see them as nasty, disgusting creatures. No so! Oh, I admit they are not very clean animals and often they can be mean, inflicting nasty bites. I have been on the receiving end of their incisors on many, many occasions. They are defensive and if not accustomed to close human contact, they can and will bite.

More frequently however, domestic rats are much more friendly than most people think. Social creatures by nature, they fit very well into our world as pets, very much like a cat or dog. The inherent problems are that they do not readily housebreak, they have poor hygiene, and their life expectancy is short. Still, many people swear by them as good pets. They can show affection and respond to commands. They are loyal creatures that have been known to defend their people from perceived threats. I knew one little girl who had a wonderful relationship with her pet rat. In fact, it slept at the foot of her bed each night. While the little girl slept, the otherwise peaceable creature would not even let mom and dad near the bed to tuck the girl in.

The point is, those pets we surround ourselves with (and admittedly, I speak of mammals and birds almost exclusively in this section), listen to us, sometimes intently. They learn to respond to commands and requests by repetition, but they also can understand and respond to what is being said the very first time.

It depends on the individual. I suspect animals are like people in that regard. Some of us are less intelligent than others. Some of us focus on different interests, so that we are motivated by some things, but slow to show interest in others. The average household pet, who has not been subjected to some sort of obedience training is no different.

Animals are also often innovative. We may ask them to fetch a ball and they wind up bringing us several. Or they may bring us something else because it is of more interest to them than the ball. Or they may not do anything at all, simply because they do not feel like it.

My dogs know what "get the ball" means. It means we are going to play. And that is a lot of work for me because two of three of my dogs like to play ball and they are very competitive. I have to throw a ball alternately for each of them to chase down, while ensuring they remain separated.

Usually they are eager to play, but once in a great while they aren't. They just want to sleep or they are busy doing something else. I know they hear me and understand, but they just aren't interested. Regardless, they do listen and understand. They have an amazing capacity for fathoming what we are saying.

Now, I am sure you understand that this does not mean that we can say to them "please go get my oxfords, third drawer of my dresser in the blue room down the hall" and expect them to be successful. There is a limit to their capacity. However, when we say "go" or "come" most pets, be they dogs, cats, horses, birds, etc., already know what is expected. It is part conditioning by repetition, but it is also part recognition of the word and understanding its meaning.

How well they interpret what follows action words depends upon how perceptive we are as to their capacity to understand and/or their desire to respond. A new puppy or kitten will not have the familiarity with words that an older animal has, but they have an eager spirit. A dog which seldom gets exercise, or an older cat, probably will be lethargic and pretty much unresponsive to most action words. They will listen and understand, but it might take a stick of dynamite to make them move. But a dog which is often tasked to learn and play will be eager to listen and respond.

Take my Westie. When I find the time to play, she is always eager and ready. She responds quickly, sometimes too quickly. I want to tell her "go get the ball", but upon hearing the word "go", she is gone, responding to the action word without waiting for the identifier. Consequently, she races through the house and comes back with the first of her toys that she encounters.

I show slight disapproval and say "no, I said go get the...", but again, before I get the word "ball" out, she hears the "go", drops whatever she is holding and again races off into toy land looking for something else.

68

If it happens to be the ball that she finds on this latest journey, all is well and the communicating ends and we play. If not the ball, I repeat the "no" again and give her a stern look. It appears to me that the gesture has the intended effect on her as she sits quietly trembling with anticipation, waiting for my next words. At least, that is how it appears to me. It may very well be that she is thinking "What an idiot - why can't he make up his mind already"?

Whatever the case may be, I take a bit of a different approach the third time. I look at her and give her the identifier first, "ball - go get the ball". In this way I know she got the spherical picture of the ball before she got the action word. As with the other times, she takes off in a flash, but this time comes back with a ball. I have spoken and she has listened, received the message and acted appropriately upon it.

We have seen this "listening" work with dogs, cats, cows, monkeys, horses, pot belly pigs and a variety of other mammals. It is communicating in the very simplest form, but it is communicating nonetheless.

I would hazard to say it is on the same level as a person from Germany speaking to a person from China, neither of them understanding the other's language. They need to communicate, but each only knows a few key words and phrases from the other's language. They are forced to rely upon gestures, tone and body language to augment the few words they know. It is usually a very funny scene to see people with different tongues trying to communicate. Often they think speaking slowly or more loudly will help. In the end, pointing and gesturing and using known words is what brings about successful communicating.

CHAPTER 3

COMMUNICATING

Though not the best example, I think it is similar to how our pets learn to communicate with us (and we with them). We do not speak each other's language, so we learn key words (or in their case sounds), learn to interpret body language and tone and somehow arrive at that point where we understand each other.

Animals may no longer possess the ability to speak, if in fact they ever had it at all, but they do still listen and understand. Their level of understanding may vary from animal to animal, but when an animal bonds with people, they most certainly are attentive when those people communicate with them. Some focus so passionately on listening that we feel inclined to hold complete conversations with them.

Cats are prone to sit and listen to their humans for long periods of time, and they often show great interest in what is being said. Readers report to me that their cat will purr when they are telling them about a pleasant experience or swish their tail the way cats do when they speak of something that bothers them. Some may attribute this to a reaction by the animal to voice inflections, but that is too convenient an explanation. There is much more substance to their reaction than a perception of mood. If it were just that, it would be evident only at the moment of exchange, but often the family pet's mood will mirror the prevailing mood in the family unit. Your world overlaps theirs. What upsets you, upsets them.

I had one wonderful old cat who would listen so intently, that I thought he was going to answer me. When I sounded glad, he seemed glad and vice versa. I know he somehow perceived my mood and reacted to it, but as anyone who has kept cats knows, they also understand your words. They are intelligent and perceptive creatures.

CHAPTER 3

COMMUNICATING

Perhaps a less impeachable example is needed. As I told you earlier, not long ago we lost one of the finest pets we have ever had, and we lost her prematurely. She was a beautiful Chihuahua, just an adorable and trusting dog. She had all the typical Chihuahua traits of being afraid of thunder (and visibly shaking when it occurred), cowering in fear when the windshield wipers came on in the car, hiding when someone new came over, and spending much time under a blanket to stay warm.

A few days after this tragic loss occurred, I was sitting in my bedroom weeping in grief. Apparently my weeping was a bit loud as my young Westie overheard me and came running into the room turning her head from side to side in that way that dogs do when they hear something that perplexes them.

Let me pause momentarily to emphasize again that this happened when my Westie was young. This puppy had never been able to refrain from the things puppies do. She bit everything that came within reach...toes, fingers, electric cords, doors, walls, etc. Her name is Missy, as I mentioned earlier, but because of her propensity for chewing things, we dubbed her "Missy the Monster". I am not exaggerating when I say she could NEVER stop biting.

Moreover, she could never sit still. It was zoom, over to the window, chew on the curtain cord, zoom back to the couch, chew on the foot connected to that man, zoom over to the edge of the carpet and chew on that. She had an endless supply of energy and a mission to chew the world into oblivion. I honestly cannot remember ever seeing her asleep or without something in her mouth that was not supposed to be there.

On this occasion however, she came into the room, took one look at me, heard this strange sound coming from her "play-friend", jumped on the bed and snuggled right up to me and licked my hands. She then looked up into my eyes and I swear, by her expression and focus, if she could have spoken, she would have said "I know you miss Pebbles. I do too. But we still have each other. Can't you be happy again. Don't cry, I love you".

She put her head in my lap and just laid there, no biting, no jumping around, nothing! She just laid still as I wept, occasionally tenderly licking my hands as I stroked her, until I finally emptied myself of tears and composed myself. She remained like this throughout the 20 minutes of my blues and never tried to leave. She also did not attempt to chew, bite or play.

The behavior was so out of character for her or for any puppy for that matter. When I spoke about the loss of our mutual friend, she listened. I mean she really listened. Oh not as if she understood...she definitely understood. Her eyes seemed to say "I know, I know". And her sober mood and placid behavior told me that she was grieving with me.

So there is no misunderstanding or doubt about the significance and uniqueness of her behavior, immediately after this encounter, she went back to being Missy the Monster and resumed her quest to chew the world apart. But for the time I needed her to listen, she did so.

They listen my friend, and they understand.

CHAPTER 4
LIFE

Perhaps the most difficult task I faced in producing this book was deciding upon the correct placement of this chapter. By the time you read this, it probably will have had several different numerical designations. I even thought to exclude it, because I know it will not be well received by everyone. But since the subject of this chapter is more crucial to my case than any other information I have given you, it was imperative that it be included.

Nevertheless, it remains a very difficult subject to address. There is more potential for skepticism here than in any other part of the book. I fully expect to suffer some ridicule over what I say, but do not welcome it. Despite that threat, I feel very strongly about the thoughts I will pass on to you here. I am certain that if I can articulate them correctly, you will be compelled to agree with most of what I have to say. This puts a big monkey on my back, for I know that you truly cannot please everyone, even when you desire to do so.

There are many aspects we could discuss on the subject of life. Probably, most everyone would prefer to be told what the meaning of life is. Perhaps my comments in Chapter 6 will help you in that regard. Others might wonder about life on other planets. Still others might be concerned about the quality of life on our own planet and related environmental issues.

Unfortunately, as important as those issues might be, they really do not fit into our theme. So we will pass on them and forge ahead to address a much larger issue. Specifically, I want to ask, and answer a question that is seldom addressed, namely "what is life"?

CHAPTER 4

LIFE

That may seem like a very elementary question, but it is one that may cause you to do a little more thinking than you may have expected to do as we progress through the answer. As you explore this issue with me, it will hopefully occur to you that this is a subject we take for granted, but one that we should thoroughly understand because it carries with it such important spiritual implications.

Let us begin our quest for this answer in a place where most of us acknowledge that human and animal life began, the Garden of Eden. Even many non-Christian cultures allude to life beginning in such a garden, so this should not be hard for most readers to agree with. It was here, according to the Bible and Christian and Jewish faiths, that God originally housed the work of his hands. We will not discuss the actual act of creation in detail as that information is more than adequately covered in a much greater book than this. Rather, let us explore the facts we know about God's plan for the living creatures he created.

God's original plan for this world was that it should be perfect...that mankind should be perfect and that we should live forever. The perfect plan also included animals, and in keeping with the longevity considerations of that plan, they too were made perfect and intended to live without ever dying. Neither people nor animals would age or suffer disease under God's plan.

Of course we know that all of that changed when man launched his own plan and disobeyed the Lord. The point we need to see is that animals were part of the big plan. In fact, they were necessary, and perhaps crucial elements to it. They were so important to the habitat of mankind that God made them first so that they would be in place when people arrived.

CHAPTER 4

LIFE

Animals were created for many reasons. The initial, and perhaps most important reason for their creation was to provide companionship to Adam, and therefore mankind. Their companionship pleased Adam and made him happy.

Lest we forget this very important fact, animals were made for God's pleasure too. God created them with his own hands and to do so brought him great pleasure. We are told that after God surveyed everything he made, he assessed it as being "very good".

We are to interpret this to mean that the animals were exactly as he wanted them to be (as if there was any doubt). It may be difficult from this side of the fall of mankind to look at wasps, ants, snakes, and skunks to see what God saw when he called very good, but originally they were.

Originally wasps did not sting and skunks did not fumigate. Back then, they were the companions of mankind. Adam and Eve embraced the creatures made by God's hand and the animals reciprocated with affection for them. Neither man nor animal ate meat. There was no killing and no death. They and the animals ate fruit and grain and vegetables.

I am not sure what they did for entertainment in the garden, but no doubt the human/animal relationship closely mirrored our relationships with our pets today. There was probably a lot of playing between them and the garden was filled with happiness and harmony.

Again, verbal communication may have been possible. I do not know that to be fact, but it sure is an intriguing possibility. If that ability was in place, I am certain that animals will have that ability restored in the future, because whatever was part of the original plan will be made to be again. God is immutable. He never changes. I will expound on that thought in a moment, but for now I think it best to return to the question at hand, "what is life"?

At the risk of sounding a little "zen" or "eastern" in my theology (and I assure you that I am not of those persuasions in even a small way), I want readers to know that there are several levels of life; or rather, several conscious states of life. Now that I see it in print, it does sound a little eastern in philosophy, but I assure you that it is not intended to give any credence to anything but Bible tenets. If you hear me out, I believe you will agree with the points I make.

If you take a moment to really think about it, there are definite differences between the various life forms found on, in and under our world. I am not speaking of the different shapes, colors, habits, etc. of the various creatures, but rather the levels of awareness and intellectual abilities of different life groups.

Let me look at each of the groups in some depth to help you understand what I mean. While there may be some insignificant overlap between these levels of awarenesses that I will define, the distinguishing borders that separate one group from the others are very well defined. These levels, discussed in detail below, are sure to draw criticism from those who do not share my view. I cannot help that. I must remain faithful to the facts of science and the teachings of the Bible.

CHAPTER 4

LIFE

Here then is the structure of non-microscopic life on our planet as I understand it. Again, I am not going to go into technical detail. I merely want to give you a brief overview of each level of life and qualify why they are higher or lower in the scale of consciousness.

Plants

I think any rational person would agree that plant life is a lower level of life than that of people. It is arguably the lowest level of life on earth. In fact, the term "life" may be an overstatement. The Bible says quite clearly that "life is in the blood". Plants do not contain blood as we define it. It seems that their level of consciousness, if they have consciousness at all, is limited to an awareness of themselves. More accurately, it is an awareness of their own needs.

I have heard people say that they talk to their plants and that the plants respond with better growth and health. I find that a very hard concept to accept. It is much rather the case that people who are conscientious enough to converse with their plants, might just be the kind of folks who attend to those plants much more proactively than others who do not. It is probable therefore, even likely, that this is the reason for the better growth and not the verbal encouragement.

There seems to be evidence that plants think, what with the way ivy climbs, carnivorous plants trap prey and tropical flora commission their seeds to populate foreign shores. We all know that appearances can be deceiving, however. I submit that these actions are simply the plant's natural and involuntary reaction to external stimuli.

When plants turn toward sunlight or a Venus Fly Trap closes and secretes digestive juices, it is because certain sensory apparatus is stimulated. I once fed a wad of paper to a Venus Fly Trap plant and it tried to process the object until I forcibly removed it the next day. As far as prolific tropical plants are concerned, such as the Mangrove, these plants drop seeds where they will as does any plant. Since Mangroves grow in or near the ocean, when seeds fall, they are carried away by the tide and deposited wherever the prevailing wind and current take them. How preposterous to imagine that Mangroves might understand currents and tides. In spite of all that, let us avoid contention on the subject by assuming that plants do indeed possess life. Obviously, they grow and reproduce, so in some sense of the word, they are alive. But is this a conscious life?

I suppose the best way to explain the point I am trying to make about different levels of consciousness is to offer that:

- plants have bodies;
- animals have bodies and souls; and
- human beings have bodies, souls and spirits

Before we can proceed any further, we must take a moment to define this word "soul" in the context I am using it. This word "soul" is translated from the Hebrew word *nephesh* over 100 times in the Old Testament. It is also used in the New Testament several dozen times as *psuche.* In ancient Greek and Hebrew, punctuation was usually absent from texts, so that one had to rely upon the context in which the word was used. So many variances were possible that it was difficult to interpret the meaning in the use unless you really rolled your sleeves up and spent time researching every word.

To give you an example of the vast application of these words, some of the translated words for "soul" are <u>breath</u>, <u>body</u>, <u>creature</u>, <u>desire</u>, <u>appetite</u>, <u>lust</u>, <u>mind</u>, to name just a few. Again, application is dependent upon contextual use. To further exacerbate the problem of application, often people who use the word "soul" are just plain lazy and do no research before using the word in some new context. Thus, they use it inappropriately. They prefer to pass along what someone else has written or said without checking the interpretation themselves.

As a consequence, there is much controversy when the word is used. Especially exasperating is when someone who misuses the word, tries to correct someone who does not. In my work of helping people who contact me with their grief, writing articles on pet loss, or serving as guest author in an internet chat room, I am occasionally confronted by alleged "Bible scholars" who want to call me on the carpet for my use of the word. Invariably, they try to give me a quick lesson in Greek or Hebrew. Believe it or not, I have even had people try to correct me by using Latin interpretations, when Latin was not a Bible language.

Admittedly, I am not a Greek or Hebrew scholar. I have taken courses and can navigate my way through those languages in study, but I am far from being proficient. Also, I do not consider myself a Bible scholar. I do not think anyone is. I consider myself extremely proficient and knowledgeable in scripture, having several New Testament books and perhaps 10,000 verses memorized, but who truly can be a "scholar" in the infinite things and thoughts of God? At best, we remain ever students at his holy feet.

CHAPTER 4

LIFE

I do not want to take time to argue the fine points of interpreting the word "soul". I completely understand the confusion people experience because of the many uses in scripture and the way many use the word. Instead, in order to avoid any controversy in my use of the word, I am going to try an approach that I think all should be able to agree upon.

The words "soul" and "spirit" are sometimes used interchangeably by people referring to scripture. Indeed, there is a relation, but there is a distinct difference as well. The word used for "soul", despite many variances, generally speaks to your "life". In other words, we *are not a soul*, we *have a soul*, or we have a life. In this sense, animals are the same as us. We both have a soul or life.

The word "spirit" is closely related, but very much different. The spirit is who we are. It is "me". We can say that we *are a spirit*, not *have a spirit*. Our spirit gives us a consciousness of God and also of our need for him. It sets us apart from animals. Animals have no need for God in the matters of redemption or reconciliation.

When people use the word "soul", almost without exception they mean that part of us that can be redeemed. For instance, how many times have we seen in a movie where someone "sold their soul to the devil". It is a misuse of the word, but one that has unfortunately been adopted into our vocabulary. I want readers to know that when I refer to that word "soul" I am actually saying "life" or "life force", if you will. I am not speaking of the spirit. Rather, I am trying to illustrate the difference between animals and humans by showing that both have a "soul" or "life", but only humans have a "spirit" or "God consciousness".

This does not mean that animals are not loved by God, nor does it mean they are not provided for by him. So many so called "scholars" try to point out, while misusing the word "soul", that animals have no hope of eternity because they have no redeemable soul. Bunk! Animals are innocents. They have no sin and are not in need of redemption. If we apply the flawed logic that since they have no soul (in the sense they are using the word) and cannot be in heaven, then we are going to have to kick out all the other beasts that are there, because they also have no need for redemption either. And we cannot stop there. The angels also have to go, for they are not partakers in salvation. For that matter, God the Father is not in need of redemption. Would they deny him place in his own kingdom? How foolish an argument.

In Job 12:10 we are told "in whose hands is the soul of every living thing". Obviously this word is inclusive of all things living. It does not differentiate. ALL are in God's hands. It does not say they are in his hands temporarily. It does not give a time limit at all. God is constant and eternal and whatever is in his hands is also eternal. Shall something die in the life-giving hands of God?

What does this tell us? Do we need to dig deeply to discover its meaning and intent as some so called "scholars" suppose. Does God hide things so that they are difficult to understand? The answer is an absolute and qualified "no". God writes simply so we can understand. He simply says that the "life" or "life force" of every living thing is in his hands or under his control. This passage does not address the redeemable creature, but rather the life or consciousness of living things in general.

It is in this sense then, that I assert that animals have a "soul". I realize that I am discussing this in the section set aside for plants, but it was necessary to make this distinction now to assist us in framing the next category of awareness properly.

Plants have only bodies. They do not have a soul or spirit. Consequently, there is no awareness of anything outside of the plant itself, if even that awareness exists. It is much more probable that auto-responses are misconstrued as conscious movement.

If I take an axe to a tree root, it does not try to dodge the axe, nor does it cry out in pain. It is not consciously aware of pain. There is no thinking process involved. If there was, it would learn not to let its roots grow so close to the surface because a madman with an axe who lives nearby will continue to attack it. But it does not.

As far as the plant knows, noting outside of itself exists. I do not mean to belittle plants, only to dispel the elevated position some suppose to give them. Plants simply do not have anything more than a body with auto-reactive capabilities.

Animals

If you were to swing that same axe at an animal (which I neither recommend nor condone), in contrast to the plant, there would be an immediate reaction. The animals would either duck, move or otherwise attempt to get out of the way of the blow. It may even counter-attack. This is because animals have a soul or life. We may even refer to it as intellect or mind, the seat of their world-consciousness.

Animals use that consciousness to be aware of their surroundings and to respond to actions by other entities in those surroundings. Granted some animals are slower witted or slower moving than others, but all would react out of a sense of self-preservation. Even an opossum would feign death to avoid being hit. The sightless bat would detect the movement of the axe with their "radar" and adjust their flight accordingly.

Animals see, hear, smell or somehow detect the danger and react to it. Unlike the plant, animals are not limited to just possessing a body. Indeed they have a body, one that is profoundly more complex and superior to that of any plant. But they have minds too, which allow them to apply reason and logic. This is a higher level of life than plants. In fact, it is an enormous jump up the scale.

Insects

This category may seem out of place if you were anticipating that I was restricting my thoughts to an escalating scale of life consciousness. I placed it here in order to avoid any confusion concerning the border between plants and animals. In an escalating scale it certainly should have been between them.

Insects represent the largest and most diverse group of living things on earth. They literally outnumber animals and people several million to one (or more). Plants give them a better run for their money per capita, but almost every plant has dozens, if not hundreds of insects living on it. Excluding the grass, I probably have 100 plants in my yard. But I am sure the insects number in the hundreds of thousands.

There isn't much we can say about insects that would enhance the purpose of this book. It is obvious that most insects use instinct more than intellect in their daily activities. Still, many apparently do have the capacity to reason. No one can deny that they are aware of their surroundings and of other living creatures, or that they also are concerned about self-preservation.

When compared to animals however, their mind, and therefore, their awareness, is extremely limited. While it would be very interesting to place insects in our study, it is not really important and I doubt anyone will much care that I exclude them. So let us move on to people.

Humans

Human beings are at a higher level of life, greater in dimension than that of animals. Like plants and animals, we have a body that gives us self-awareness. This self-awareness is superior to both plants and animals in many ways, as we are able to better ourselves, achieve,and accomplish.

We have a soul or mind that is without question superior to any animal. It gives us an awareness of ourselves, as well as an awareness of other human beings, animals and our surroundings in the physical world. However, it reaches beyond the apprehension of animals in that we look to the stars beyond as our realm of physical awareness. Animals do not.

Then, unique to humans, we have a spirit, which gives us an awareness of the supernatural and the unknown. Humans alone possess the capacity to perceive God, to worship an unseen Deity and to think and plan for life beyond this physical life.

I understand that there exists a general consensus that animals have a supernatural perception. We have all grown up under the assumption that animals have some sort of sixth sense. And truthfully, sometimes it appears they do. We hear tales of dogs seeing ghosts or other apparitions that we cannot see ourselves, of their hair standing up on their backs for no apparent reason, of horses stampeding out of their stalls or barns before an earthquake occurs, or of any countless other stories of that genre.

As a lad growing up in Hawaii, I remember well a story told to me by my brother-in-law. He told me how he and some other fellows had been out pig hunting in the mountains near Kolekole pass - the place traditionally acknowledged as where the first wave of Japanese fighter planes came through in their attack on Pearl Harbor.

He continued with the story, telling me that as they came upon a grove of trees, their dogs stopped dead in their tracks and howled at something that the men could not see. My brother-in-law swore that there was nothing to be seen...that there was nothing obstructing their view in the direction the dogs were looking.

The story gets a little nauseating here. I apologize for what I share with you next, but it is necessary for you to understand the story. The men, observing old Hawaiian folklore, took the makapiapia (Hawaiian word for the "yuk" that collects in the corner of an eye) from their dog's eyes and wiped it in their own eyes. This, according to legend, allowed them to see what the dogs saw. And what they say they saw was a giant "ghost pig". Not just a ghost pig, but a giant one at that.

When I hear stories like this, I have to say "pass the bread the bologna has already been around". I do not mean to disrespect my brother-in-law in any way, but rather emphasize how people sensationalize the natural abilities of animals and assign a supernatural sense to them that they simply do not possess.

As a person who spends a lot of time in the wild and around animals, I can tell you that it certainly does appear that animals possess some sort of special sense. I believe there is another explanation, however. Isn't it more likely that their ability to sense earthquakes just before they happen and their reaction to things that seem to not be there can be credited to their very keen senses of smell, hearing, sight, etc.?

In other words, a horse running in panic several moments before we feel a quake is really a reaction to the horse's keen sense of hearing rather than some extrasensory perception. The rumbling deep in the earth was there for us to hear, but because our hearing is inferior, we could not hear it as readily as the horse.

Animals have better senses than humans (and sometimes just plain better sense too). I think that it would surprise you to know just how much superior to our sense of smell the ability of a dog is. Before I performed some research on the subject, I would have thought that a dog's sense of smell was perhaps five times better than the average human. I could even probably have believed it was ten times more efficient. In fact, to my utter surprise, I learned that most household dogs have a sense of smell 30,000 times better than ours.

To put that in terms that provide more impact, let's say you entered a house where someone wearing perfume had just been visiting. The person had already left, but there was a faint wisp of perfume still in the air. You picked up on the sweet bouquet because there were still thousands of perfume particles in the air.

A week later, you have an opportunity to visit the house again and there is absolutely no trace of the perfume. The number of particles remaining in the air is almost zero, and you cannot detect even a whiff of it. But your dog can still smell it.

If that gap in abilities is not enough to stagger you, try this...it is reported that bloodhounds, which are bred and used by design for searching by smell, have nearly three times the ability of smell that the average household dog possesses. A bloodhound's sense of smell is 80,000 times greater than yours and mine.

Conceivably, a bloodhound could smell a golf ball at a driving range for say 2 seconds, the ball be hit out into the range among thousands of other golf balls, the dog released to find it, and successfully find that one ball without error. Sound too easy? Then try this remarkable true story on for size.

A young girl was abducted by a stranger in a van, driven about 12 miles away and held captive in the van on a deserted road. It was later learned that the van did not stop once while traveling from the point of abduction to the deserted road 12 miles away.

CHAPTER 4

LIFE

Several hours after the abduction, the local authorities gave their bloodhound a piece of the child's clothing for reference and put the dog on the trail. It took several more hours, but that dog led police on foot down the same 12 miles of highway transited by the van, off the same exit ramp and down the same deserted road. The bloodhound led them right to the van and the victim was rescued unharmed.

The handler estimated that the scent of the girl coming out of the van while passing at a normal rate of speed was perhaps one part in several billion, which means it was almost indistinguishable. Yet, the animal picked it up and sorted it out from all the other airborne odors, including the exhausts of all the thousands of vehicles that had passed by during the several hours of searching.

Was it some sort of sixth sense the dog was employing? No, it was not. He just possessed and employed far superior equipment than we humans have.

Humans on the other hand, do possess a sixth sense of sorts. Like animals, the average human being has the basic five senses. Ours are not as sharp as those of animals, but they are more than adequate and give us the wherewithal to operate and exist within the physical confines of our world. Unlike the animals however, we have an additional ability to perceive or sense something beyond the physical limits of our world. I have labeled this sense "SONG", which simply is an acronym for our ability to "Sense Our Need of God". Animals lack this ability, probably because they do not need it. They are innocent creatures who have a standing with God from their creation. They need no redemption or reconciliation.

I could be wrong, but I just do not see an awareness of God in animals. Please do not misconstrue my words to mean that they do not have a relationship with him, for he tells us that they do. They apparently just do not seem to be aware of it at the present. For instance, you will see birds building a nest, but never a temple. You will see beavers building a dam, but never an altar. Someone might teach a dog the "trick" of folding their paws and bowing their head, but this does not qualify as praying and their incentive is a treat rather than worship.

Humans alone have this awareness of God. Admittedly, there are those who no longer recognize it, but that is their choice or the result of a hard, sinful lifestyle. They, like every person ever to live, once were aware of their SONG, but have cast aside the need they felt or purposely ignored it.

Those folks are few. It may seem sometimes like atheists run rampant in our country and world, but the numbers favor those who believe in some sort of supernatural deity. In every culture, even those where the populace is oppressed and human rights appear to be non-existent, where religious beliefs are forbidden, the sense lives on. It is something placed inside of each of us by our creator.

Our SONG sets us apart from the animals and confounds the evolutionists (because even they feel that need inside themselves). You can believe what you will, but not one of us can honestly deny that sense in our heart and mind that someone is out there watching us, that everything is just too perfect to have just happened.

CHAPTER 4

LIFE

As I stated earlier, the Bible says that life is in the blood, or, to put it in other words, blood is needed to sustain the life of our body. The essentialness of its life-sustaining properties should not need validation. Every person in control of their faculties has demonstrated that they subscribe to this ideal when they react to a simple cut. Let anyone accidentally break the thin layer of epidermis that holds back their blood, and their immediate and total attention is focused on closing the breech, to the exclusion of almost everything else. Few matters take higher precedence with us than preserving our blood, because we know that therein is our life. When it runs out, so too does our life.

How the entire mechanism of our circulatory system works and how that blood affects and effects life, who can say with certainty. Science can break down the parts and say "it works and here is why", but they are looking at the result rather than the cause.

It is so much more complicated than that. Science can tell us everything about the parts of the blood, but when it comes to explaining how it is that our life is somehow in the blood, not many scientists step forward to speak. The only sure position is to acknowledge that life is of, from and in God, just like his word says. He wills it and he alone sustains it.

In a sense then (and this is where I hope you allow me some latitude and do not misconstrue my comments to be influenced by eastern philosophy), God is life. When I consider all the facts of the preceding paragraphs, I must conclude that God is not only the source of life, but, since he alone has the power to make it, to control it, and to sustain it, he is effectively life himself.

He is the "life force" if you will. He existed before anyone or anything else alive existed. The record he gave us of the beginning of life states clearly that "he breathed life" into us. Hence, whatever life we have, it originated with God and nowhere else, especially not in a swamp (for even the swamp did not exist).

God is original life. The fact that life is now reproduced automatically and naturally does not diminish the fact that life exists because he wills and allows it to. To put it in the real context that I want to convey, God is life and we are sort of "little chips" of his life. I hope that makes sense to you, because I have over-tasked my mind (you know, the one I previously claimed was so much superior to that of animals) searching for the best way to explain it. I want to say it more clearly, but that is going to have to suffice.

If you are still onboard and haven't jumped ship on me yet, I need to sum up all I have said to make my point about what life is absolutely clear. In light of the fact that God is life and all life stems from him, it only makes sense for us to conclude that irrespective of what happens to a living creature on this earth, the life or spirit of that creature can never and will never end. It is connected to the eternal God.

And as I search the scripture, God never created a temporal creature. Even Satan, great embodiment of evil that he is, will live forever and not be annihilated or extinguished. It is true that he will live in the judgment God has already pronounced upon him and never see heaven, but he will live on.

How presumptuous for men (and women) to think that God would spare an evil being like Satan from annihilation, but visit it upon such innocent and wonderful creatures as animals. That is not God's way. That principle is foreign to the Word of God. He did not create just to destroy.

If you are still with me, I need just a bit more latitude to bring these thoughts home. While it is my strong conviction that all life is in God's hands, and therefore cannot and will not end, equally strong is my conviction that there is a very big difference between animal and human life in regards to eternity.

For human beings, we all know, to varying degrees, that eternal rest and co-existence with God depends upon reconciliation through the savior he provided (it is his plan, not mine - it is from His Book). Many will enjoy that rest and fellowship as believers, while many others, we are told, will spend their eternal life in a place not quite as restful. The record of God's reconciliatory act can be believed or rejected. The choice is up to the individual.

If my stating that offends you, I am truly sorry. However, I can no more shade the truth to that than I can to any other of the truths I have shared with you in this book. Truth is truth whether we personally believe it or not. God gives a very easy to understand plan for reconciliation with him in his word. The reason I bring this up at all is because there exists a spiritual quandary regarding animal and human afterlife, and if I did not make an effort to specifically point it out, some might miss it altogether.

Animals have no need for redemption, as I have already shown. It follows that they are therefore, not subject to judgment in any sense of the word. Their eternity is sure. To see that in God's Word is thrilling to my heart. It eliminates any guesswork or erroneous thinking.

Conversely, people are in need of reconciliation. Our eternity is sure, but our destination may not be. Therein lies the quandary. I can affirm that animals are safe and their future sure, but I do not want anyone thinking I can give them the same assurance for themselves. I have not that authority. Nor would I be so presumptuous. That is an individual responsibility between each person and God. Many try to meet God on their terms, but the truth is, He demands we meet him on his terms, coming to him through his son (John 14:6).

I do not know how better to state that. I tried to be as inoffensive and unassuming as I could be. Some think I should say nothing at all, but that is not an option. What kind of a person would I be to bring hope and comfort to someone about their departed pet and not share with them the whole truth?

CHAPTER 5
THE MILLENNIUM

Before you flip past this chapter, let me assure you that I am not going to load you down with a lot of scripture. I understand that there is good probability that some readers do not share my love for the scriptures or my same faith in the Lord. I know that this would cause you to have a low tolerance level for someone quoting scripture, so I will refrain from doing so.

You will have to allow me some latitude however, in order for me to complete my case on animal afterlife. This "millennium", or 1,000 year period provides some pertinent insight into the world and lives of animals that I do not think we can ignore. As there is only one source that talks about this last period of time before cataclysmic, eschatological events take place that will change our earth forever, I need to make several references to the information it offers.

Both the Old Testament and New Testament make reference to this greatly anticipated period of Jesus' earthly reign (this is where the term "King of Kings" actually applies in scripture and history). After this 1,000 years of the theocracy he establishes, he destroys the old earth and heaven (atmosphere around the earth and what we call outer space) and creates the new earth. It would be so easy for me to get sidetracked here to go into greater detail about these events, but I will restrain myself from doing so and address only the things that apply to our study.

Paraphrasing some of the scriptural insights, the Bible tells us that the "wolf shall dwell with the lamb, the leopard with the kid, the cow with the bear, their young ones shall lay down together and the lion shall eat straw like the ox".

CHAPTER 5
THE MILLENNIUM

Clearly, there will no longer be predator and prey. Moreover, there shall no longer be a schism between the animal and human world. Again, scripture says of the previously wild beasts, "and a child shall lead them" and "a child shall put his hand on the hole of the asp and the den of the cockatrice" (legendary offspring of a chicken and serpent in ancient Europe, more currently and correctly translated to be an adder).

The implication is unmistakable. During this period, animals will return to their first and intended estate of companion. They will not be carnivorous and we will have no need to fear them, or they us. There will no longer be wild beasts. Rather, all shall be domesticated. It appears that this will prevail throughout the animal kingdom, among mammals, reptiles, birds, etc.

Even more profound, they, and humans, shall live without death for the entire 1,000 year period. Since all living things will be herbivorous during this period, a great demand will be placed on the plant kingdom, already significantly decimated by the cataclysmic events foretold in scripture. I have to assume that since life will be prolonged, and the population increasing rapidly without natural attrition, conditions for growth of vegetation will be changed to produce optimal crops during this period. In fact, one might reason that since God will re-establish animals and people in their original relationship, he might well re-establish the original garden conditions, but on a much larger scale.

Imagine the wonder of no death, no unrest, no environmental disasters, no draught or flood, but rather harmony in nature and an incorruptible theocracy where perfect and pure judgments are rendered. It shall be a grand time.

CHAPTER 5
THE MILLENNIUM

Now then, in this picture of eternity we call the millennium, we have a reconfirmation of God's original plan for the life he created. After the millennium, there is nothing left to happen in our present universe. That is not to say that everything ends. Quite the contrary. We are told that this signifies the beginning of eternity for the life God created. We just are not told what happens after the universe we occupied for so long comes to an end.

A lot of very big things happen during this last 1,000 years, but once it is over, it is over and those things are never experienced again. We enter the realm without time, that place called "eternity". This is where God has always existed and now we become a part of it. Again, we are not told what will happen specifically, but we are told that all his creatures will enjoy this new relationship and life with their creator.

The animals, in confirmation of God's original plan for them, have been changed back to their original state during the millennium. They live without death or fear, the way God had originally planned for them to be. This is not a change, per se, but a change back. The original plan, as we noted earlier, was interrupted temporarily by man, and not by God's will or desire.

It would appear then that God's efforts of reconciliation of mankind to himself have come full circle since the fall. Faith will have been replaced with sight. In other words, mankind's former position with God will have been restored and everything set right again, the way it was intended to be. Believers will be with God. So to, the evidence indicates, his original plan for animals has also come full circle, and they are once again as they were intended to be.

CHAPTER 5
THE MILLENNIUM

I think I have built a solid case. However, let me offer some additional thoughts for you to consider. As usual, no individual thought is enough to convince, but the sum of evidence adds up to an overwhelming proof that God does care about more than just us humans.

Creatures we now refer to as animals, were put in the garden with mankind. They were created before we were created. They were not an afterthought, but a forethought. They were and remain important. God did not make them temporary creatures, but intended rather that they should live forever. Nothing has been written to suggest that God has changed his mind.

When the earth was destroyed by flood (by the way, almost every ancient culture historically references a world-wide flood), God preserved the animals along with mankind. When the flood subsided, God made a covenant with Noah to never destroy the earth again by flood. God extended this covenant to the animals. Obviously, God's lesser creatures (those not made in his image) are equally important to him.

There is more. When Jesus was born, who did God the Father have present, people or animals? Of course Mary and Joseph had to be there, but there were no other people at the birth. Others came later, but they were not at the birth. Yet, present were many from the animal kingdom. I will offer a more in depth explanation of this in the upcoming sequel, but suffice it to say here that God found it acceptable for his son to be born in the presence of his innocent creatures.

CHAPTER 5
THE MILLENNIUM

Another momentous example of God's pleasure with his creatures is seen in the account of Jesus' fasting in the wilderness. We are told so very little about this period of Jesus' life, but what we are told is significant. Having retired away from his followers, to fast in the wilderness for 40 days, it is offered that he spent the time with the wild beasts.

How interesting is this, that Jesus chose to dwell among the creatures he had created during a very solemn time of his ministry? How exciting to see the importance of animals in so many major historical events.

When we couple these stand alone examples of God's comfortableness with his creatures with the picture of tameness we are given of their millennial existence, certainly we must conclude that they are important to God. We must acknowledge that animals are in it for the long haul and not just hitching a ride through our earthly history.

One scripture I have to offer to cap off this chapter is found in **Revelation 5:13**. If you have believed nothing else I have said about the eternity of animals, let this passage grip you. Study it out and try your best to make it say something other than what I offer you below. I assure you that you will not be able to do so. It says:

"And every creature which is in heaven, and on the earth, and under the earth, and such as are in the sea, and all that are in them, heard I saying, blessing and honor, and glory, and power, be unto him that sitteth upon the throne, and unto the lamb for ever and ever".

THE MILLENNIUM

Wow! What more proof do we need? God, who cannot lie and who does not make mistakes, records that every creature was heard to praise him. In my mind, **"EVERY"** is an all-inclusive term meaning **"all"**. So **ALL** creatures is what John (the writer used to pen this book of Revelation) is referring to. Not part, not some, not many, not just those that existed at the time of this writing, but ALL creatures.

It also said of every creature, "which is in heaven", indicating strongly that some animals had passed on but still lived. One might argue that this refers only to animals whose only life was in heaven, and that would not be out of context at all. But the rest of the verse seems to cover every conceivable place animals could be whether dead or alive, and this cannot be explained away without deliberate misinterpretation.

Finally, again, it says "and **ALL** that are in them". This leaves little room to question just how many animals this includes. An acquaintance of mine gave me the best definition of this world "all" that I have ever heard. He said "**all** means **all** and that is **all all** means". The intent seems clear and unchallengeable to me...that **ALL** creatures, animal, human, living or dead, are important to God and are eternal creatures.

John wrote that all creatures would one day worship and praise God. This is one of the major themes of the Bible, that God created mankind to worship and adore him. We may get pre-occupied with ourselves and our lives, but worship of God is what he created us for. Some may not like to hear that. It may not fit into their theology, or it may be offensive to them, but that does not mitigate the purpose of God. I would simply ask "who gave life to whom"? Then whose opinion really matters?

God's desire is that all of his creation worship and praise him. That includes not only humans, who are made in his image, but the lesser creatures which were made by his almighty hand. In fact, there are places in the scripture where God says even inanimate objects like the rocks will praise him. So when God says "all", I think we should concede that he knew what he was saying and meant it.

God cares about his creation. He loves all the creatures made by his hand. He has made provision for them all. And I speak not only of earthly provision. The Lord tells us that he clothes the lilies of the field and keeps an eye on the sparrow. He oversees the lives of animals on this earth, directing their seasonal migrations and ensuring they have enough to eat. But he also cares about their eternity. Remember what we read in the Book of Job about the soul of every living thing being in his hands.

I think it is interesting to note that not only does the last book written in the Bible (Revelation) make reference to the eternity of animals, but also the book first written, Job (Genesis appears first in the Old Testament and is chronologically first in history, but Job was penned first). We see that this book gives testimony to the care God shows his creatures.

We can conclude that in God's entire revelation to mankind, from beginning to end, he emphasizes the importance of animals, not to us, but to him! Given that God is the only constant in our universe, given that he declares himself immutable, how can anyone be so presumptuous as to think God would change his mind about his animals?

CHAPTER 6
SOME FINAL THOUGHTS

I hope this book has proven to be a tremendous help to you. As I pointed out earlier, my goal was singular...to give comfort to those in need. I wanted that help to provide emotional benefit to you, but it was necessarily also spiritual in nature. I wanted to reach beyond any help this old world could offer and give readers the comfort that their animals are alive and well, and also a hope of seeing them again.

I don't care about sales or gaining fame. For me, being a successful author is secondary to being a helpful Christian. My desire is to help others by providing trustworthy answers to the questions that accompany loss of a pet. To that end, I want to emphasize one final time that this book is not speculative, except in those areas where I was careful to point out that I was expressing opinion rather than fact. And even then, I based my opinion upon some very solid principles.

My training in Bible doctrine, apologetics and rules of exegesis have been mentioned sufficiently to validate that my research and conclusions were not flippant, but well-thought out. Additionally, I think my candid and open approach reflects my honesty, and hopefully my integrity as well. I would rather perish than misrepresent the Word of God.

There is no doubt but that animals are eternal creatures, like all the other creatures God made. To think otherwise is to take an unsupportable and baseless position that is contrary to his word. Moreover, to hold that animals will simply cease to exist or be annihilated both minimizes the worth of these wonderful personalities and makes God out to be a villain.

CHAPTER 6
SOME FINAL THOUGHTS

It is simply preposterous to say that God, who created them and gave them life, including personalities, emotions and the ability to reason, did so only to destroy them in the end. This would mean that he not only made a mistake in creating them, but that he does indeed change his mind, which in turn makes him as flawed as you or I. And if that were true, than what keeps him from changing his mind about you and me?

If we place our trust in him and he suddenly and whimsically changed his mind about his love for us based upon how we lived, where would that leave us? I assure you, considering my own inconsistent Christian deportment, I would be in a very leaky boat. Thank God he is not like me, but he is constant and immutable. Thank God we can depend upon him and do not have to depend upon ourselves.

God has not changed his mind about the animals. He has made provision for them. In truth, they really are his animals, and not ours. They belong to the one who created them and gave them life. They are merely on loan to us, and as inconceivable as it may seem, God loves them more than you and I ever could.

You and I would do anything we could to provide for our best friends. If we could extend their lives by just a day, we would spare no expense. Alas, we have no power over life or death. God also would do anything to provide for his animals. In fact, he does. Unlike us, God does have power and authority over life and death. He not only feeds, clothes and provides for animals in this life in ways we are not even aware of, but when our pets pass and we are helpless to do anything but grieve, God ushers them into eternity, safe in his care.

CHAPTER 6
SOME FINAL THOUGHTS

I believe that with all my heart. I would never say anything with this much gravity if I were not absolutely certain of what I was claiming. I have never said anything just because I thought it was what someone wanted to hear. People need to hear the truth. They want to hear the truth. In this case, the truth just happens to be the thing we wanted to hear.

I have almost concluded my thoughts and presentation on the topic of animal afterlife. I hope that what has been said thus far has helped you. I said in the beginning that you might start this book a skeptic. If you did, I hope that what I have given you has provoked you to a new understanding of what life is and how very important it is to the one who gives it to his creatures. This was a very key objective for me. Like the famed Billy Sunday, my ministry springs from Isaiah 61:1, in particular that portion that admonishes me to "**bind the broken-hearted**".

As important as that goal is, there is an even more important point that I am compelled to discuss, one that I have put off until now. My service to you will be incomplete if I do not take the time to address it here. Yet, I hesitate, because I know what I have to say may not sit well with some. I hope you will understand that I have no choice in this matter.

As I said above, I am compelled to speak of this. I am acutely aware that some will accuse me of preaching, but my intent is not to preach, but to fulfill my promise and complete my task of bringing you hope. The truth is a funny thing. If you only give half the story, it really is not the truth, but rather a lie. I will not lie. Accordingly, to use the term a very great American has coined, I want to give you the rest of the story.

CHAPTER 6
SOME FINAL THOUGHTS

And the rest of the story is this...I can assure you that our beloved best friends are safe and well in the presence of their creator. They no longer suffer. They no longer are subject to the ills they endured in this world. If there was brief pain associated with their passing, that pain is not even a memory for them now. It, along with the rudimentary shortcomings of this world is far removed from their new life. This I know without doubt, by faith in the solid evidence offered by the Bible.

I am absolutely sure of this when it comes to these wonderful creatures God made and loves. I can, in a sense, speak for them, and report that they live. However, I can not make the same claim for people, and that is the rest of the truth I am compelled to give you.

As I said at the beginning of this book, animals do not need faith, because they do not need reconciliation. According to the same Bible we used to establish this truth, it says people are not so. People do need faith and reconciliation. It is between them and God and I have no authority, nor have I the ability to know who has placed faith in God or not.

If I could pass along my faith to you, I would do so without hesitation. Unfortunately, faith comes from within, not without. Faith is something generated by the individual. The best I can do is to try to explain faith from a Bible perspective for you without being offensive. Without a personal faith in the Lord, we are told that we have no place in his presence. Since I do not know if you have met with the Lord on his terms, I cannot assure you about your own spiritual condition. I have neither the authority nor the right to do so.

CHAPTER 6
SOME FINAL THOUGHTS

Jesus said "I am the way, the truth and the life, no man (or woman) cometh unto the father but by me". The measure then is that God's reconciliation with you is dependent upon your coming to him through the work that the Son did. I read that verse over and over again and nowhere does it mention me as the one who decides your spiritual condition. It is between you and God and no one else.

If you are angry with me for having said all that, consider this. I never mentioned your name. I do not even know you. If you are upset with the verse I just quoted, maybe you should consider who wrote it. I assure you these are not my words. I merely quoted from a far more superior book. I suggest you take your concerns to its author. Don't be angry with me.

I realize some will still say I was too strong or too preachy in what I said above. I cannot help that. I carefully selected my words to be both kind and provoking. What kind of a person would I be, if knowing the whole truth, I only told you the half? There is too much of that in the world already and I want no part of it.

Please believe me when I say that I had no ulterior motive in making this final case. It was for your good and your good only that I presented it at all. I gain nothing by exposing myself to the ire and ridicule of those who disagree with the Bible. I provide the PETGATE e-mail address for those who have additional questions or have a need to talk with someone who understands, but some have chosen to use it to admonish me for caring about their spiritual condition.

CHAPTER 6
SOME FINAL THOUGHTS

Moving on to a completely different topic, I purposely avoided issues involving the psychological recovery process of grief. Although I have a lot of experience counseling grieving people, I am not legally qualified to do so. Moreover, even if my credentials were recognized and accepted by appropriate authorities, there would be no need for me to exercise them. There already exists an abundance of excellent literature on the subject, and an army of professionals to assist you. I could add nothing new.

Ideally, it would be best if we never suffered pet loss. Unfortunately, on this earth, the only way that you could accomplish this would be to refrain from having pets altogether. For me, and I imagine many others like me, this would be a fate worse than enduring a loss.

People like me have no alternative. We are pet and animal lovers. Our lives would be empty without their wonderful personalities and love. They are the most unassuming, uninhibited creatures God ever made. They don't care if you are in a bad mood or if you didn't have time to shower. They just want to be near you, to purr in your lap, to fill your room with their chirping, to bang a dent in the wall with their happy tail.

The people in your life all play different roles, each important in its own way and right. Your mother, a friend, the boss, your spouse...each of them are an intricate part of your life. Each of them influenced and impacted your life. If any of them had not played their part, you may not have realized that something was missing, but it would have been missing nonetheless.

CHAPTER 6
SOME FINAL THOUGHTS

The same holds true with our pets. They play an extremely important role in our life. So even though abstinence from keeping a pet may seem like a sure way to not suffer loss, in fact, you would have suffered loss already. For those of us who are hooked, there is no alternative anyway.

Given that we understand that keeping pets eventually leads to the misfortune of losing them, there are some precautions we can take to ensure their best possible longevity and quality of life. It begins with selecting our pet. Whether it be a kitten, puppy, parakeet, rabbit, hamster or whatever, we want to select an animal that appears to be healthy.

Now, I know there are some people out there who purposely seek out sick and dying animals to make a loving home for them before they pass. I do not mean to belittle your efforts or cause anyone so inclined to reconsider. We need people like you. Rather, our animal friends need people like you. You are their heroes and heroines. My gratitude is extended to you on behalf of all those who cannot thank you.

My suggestions here are meant for those who do not know much about animals or for those who are not prepared to deal with an animal that is ill or potentially ill from the start. These folks need to be careful. Acquiring an animal that has overwhelming needs that you cannot meet will usually mean that animal will suffer more and not get the care it needs from someone else who is more prepared and able to deal with the medical issue. Please avoid that situation. Consider the animal's needs first before you make a decision.

Be careful of quick attachments as well. I know those big brown eyes can just grab you and make your mind up for you. Once you are smitten, you are smitten. It doesn't matter if the animal is missing a leg or has green fur...if you have fallen for it, you have fallen. So exercise caution. There is no known remedy for "smittenitis". I give this advice out as a hypocrite, for I have suffered from the disease myself. In fact, my case is chronic.

If, however, you are not overwhelmed by the purring or snuggling or wrinkly little nose and you can maintain some semblance of composure and restraint, it would do you well to check the animal over as thoroughly as possible. I admit that this takes a fair amount of detachment and coolness, which can lead to guilt. I even feel a bit guilty writing these words, but the goal here is to give the animal the best home and the best chance. Accordingly, if you cannot handle the ailments and associated medical expenses, or if you are not prepared for the possible early loss of that animal to its ailment, I suggest you take the time to look over and choose your pet carefully.

Here are some questions you might ask yourself before making up your mind. This is not a complete list, nor is it scientific. You may want to add to the list depending on what you want the animal for (i.e. breeding, shows, mascot, etc.). So tailor your checklist to your personal needs as well as the needs of the animal.

1. Is there any obvious discolored or missing fur, feathers?
2. Lift the tail. Are hookworms present or signs of diarrhea?
3. Does the stomach area seem bloated? (indicating worms)
4. Does the animal appear lethargic or weak?

5. Is the animal's voice raspy or hoarse when they bark, etc.?
6. Is the animal able to follow hand movement without problem?
7. Are there any visible defects (i.e. limping, missing hair, etc.)?
8. Does the animal appear to have equilibrium problems?

This is not a complete list by any means, but if any of these problems exist, chances are you will have to make some big decisions. There are a lot of other things you could look for depending upon the type of pet you are seeking. I restricted my comments and checklist to small mammals and birds, but easily these same principles may be applied to just about any creature. If you are unfamiliar with the animal, obtain literature and read, read, read, before you make a decision. The more you know, the better for you and the animal.

Once you have completed your tailor-made checklist and satisfied yourself that the animal you are considering is a good fit for your lifestyle, you should consider enlisting the help of a professional to give a more quantitative medical evaluation. However you acquire your pet, whether a gift or purchase, or if it just shows up on your doorstep, you should have the animal looked over by a veterinarian. I don't want to sound like your mother (or mine), but better safe than sorry. Often, if you catch an ailment early, its negative effects can be held to a minimum.

A quick look-see by the doctor or other professionals will usually cost between $25-40, but it could save you thousands, and a lot of anxiety and grief. For that minimal cost they will perform a sort of mini-physical examination. Essentially, they will give it a quick visual once-over (yes, I know you already did that), look into the eyes, ears, nose, mouth and the other, southern end as well.

They will nod and "umm-hmmm" and usually tell you that everything looks fine. In those instances where they are not as confident that everything looks fine, they may suggest blood work or other tests. But again, it is better to catch any potential ailment early.

It may be a good practice to enter at least a verbal agreement with the breeder or pet store owner that you are going to have the animal checked by a veterinarian and if something serious is discovered, they agree to pay for the remedy. Or, if they are unwilling to do that, that they agree to take the animal back and refund your money. Speaking strictly from a business perspective, that is only fair. You are not asking them to pay for the medical examination, and you are not asking them to guarantee the animal for life. You just want to make sure they are not pulling a fast one on you.

Then, in those rare cases where something serious is discovered and greater expense is certain, you can ask the seller to foot the bill, or, that failing, ask them to refund your money. Now, in the final analysis, the seller may not honor the verbal agreement. If this happens, you will have to weigh your moral and legal options and do as your heart dictates.

If it were me, I would simply absorb the cost myself. In fact, let me completely expose my hypocrisy by telling you that each of my 3 current animals had some sort of defect when I acquired them. It didn't matter. I was hooked in minutes. How can anyone look in those loving and lonely eyes and deny them. They seem to say "Here I am, here I am, take me, take me - I don't like this place, let me come to your house".

CHAPTER 6
SOME FINAL THOUGHTS

So I am a hypocrite. I am quick to give sound advice, but I come up short when it comes to taking it. Each of my buddies were medically defective and unwanted by anyone else. They lacked the luster that perhaps medically sound animals possess, but I took them and all the responsibilities that went with them anyway. And as I think of the joy we have brought each other, I don't think it much matters.

Returning to my thoughts concerning an initial medical examination...most states require (and common sense dictates) that your animals receive certain vaccinations each year. Since you already have to pay for the office visit, what is a few dollars more to check for parasitical invaders or abnormalities?

Don't be a cheapskate when it comes to your pet. Just because your dog remains in a fenced yard and never wanders into the woods or city, don't think disease cannot reach them. I have had so many letters from people who felt their animal was safe in their little townhouse yard. They decided not to get a Parvo vaccination. They saved a few dollars, but would have probably paid 100 times that to have their best friend back.

There is a lot of responsibility associated with a pet. Canines and felines need vaccinations. Not just Rabies, but Parvo, Distemper, Kennel Fever, and sometimes more. Birds need clipping and exact diets. We could list a variety of animals and their needs if we had both room and time. Suffice it to say, the expense of maintaining a healthy pet can become significant. The dividends are usually a longer, healthier life. Conversely, a lack of proper medical regimen can spell a shorter, unhealthy life. If you cannot afford to take care of an animal, you should never take it home.

111

CHAPTER 6
SOME FINAL THOUGHTS

Another important consideration impacting upon health and longevity is diet. A good diet is essential to growth, appearance, health and long life. I feel like such a fool addressing this topic for I am the biggest offender of ensuring a good diet for my pets.

I know that good nutrition, correct portions and little junk food are paramount to good health in our pets, but I am a pushover. They have my number...I am an easy mark and they know it. My wife can sit and eat a meal and tune out the begging dog. Funny thing, but it is interesting to note that the begging dog tunes her out too. They know she is not going to budge. So, they turn their attention to me, the "mark". And I crumble and start handing out my meal. To quote comedian Lou Costello, an old friend from my hometown who is no longer with us, "I am a baaaaaad boy".

Cats are just as bad, or worse. I cannot have cats any longer since my wife developed an allergy for their fur, but most of us know that when it comes to being finicky, cats have it all over dogs. If you don't give them what they want, not only will they turn their noses up to it, but when you are not looking, they will hunt it down and help themselves to something more to their liking.

Please do not indict me for ruining my dog's diet. My intentions are the best. I purchase any number of solid, scientific diet plans. I spare no cost. It's the dogs' fault. They won't eat it. I buy it, I put it in their bowl, I tell them it is good for them. I even pretend to eat it myself and add a very convincing "ummmmmm" to the presentation. But they just won't eat it.

CHAPTER 6
SOME FINAL THOUGHTS

Fortunately, my saving grace here is that very probably you are as guilty as I am in this matter, aren't you? Sure you are. You know you are. So, how about if we determine together that we are going to start our pets on a healthier diet. Let's agree that we are going to be strong and resolute and not give in to the merciless tactics of our pets that deprive us of our dinners.

Finally, we need to exercise our animals. That may be difficult if you keep birds or fish, but if you give those types of pets enough room, they will exercise themselves. Cats usually stay in fairly good shape on their own, but I have seen some that appeared to be runaway balloons from a parade. Dogs are much easier to exercise because most of them love to play and run. They will chase just about anything you throw for them until they tire of doing so. I have also found that if you give a dog a swimming pool or a small pond, there is no end to the exercise they will get.

I regularly exercise my dogs and it shows in their appearance and in their general good health. Perhaps that is why I don't feel so very guilty about the junk food I sometimes give to them. They just do not sit around all day doing nothing. They have access to the back yard anytime they want to go - and they chase up and down the fence after squirrels, rabbits, leaves, and sometimes absolutely nothing at all.

What's more, the more they exercise, the more they want to exercise. My Westie and I play fetch the ball daily. I throw it and she fetches it some 35 times or more. I put the ball aside thinking we are done and she seems to agree with me, to a point. She thinks "yes, we are done fetching....THE BALL...but we have so many other toys here to fetch".

CHAPTER 6
SOME FINAL THOUGHTS

So then she brings me her chew toy, and then the pull socks, and then this and that, until finally we have gone through her entire inventory of toys. Finally, she tires of fetching altogether and lays down. I start toward my easy chair and she quickly jumps up and play-growls "arrraff", which means "not so fast - we haven't played the pull game yet". And so, she goes through the entire inventory again and presents me with each article in it.

If I sound as if I am complaining, I am not. I actually enjoy spending time with my dogs and expending energy along with them. It keeps us both in shape and enhances their quality and quantity of life. If you keep pets, don't confine them to a small cage or tie them to a tree all day, every day. Get outside with them and play and run and enjoy each other. Give them something exciting to look forward to each day.

Make every day count. Love them and treat them well while they are with you. They aren't with us nearly long enough. Don't ever trap yourself into wasting time you could spend with them now and regretting it later. We will see them again, but that might be a very long time.

CHAPTER 7
STORIES OF HUMOR AND SUBSTANCE

I sincerely hope this book has found its mark in your heart and manifested itself in the form of hope and encouragement. If it has, you are now equipped with the wherewithal to handle the pain and emptiness that you once could not cope with. The uncertainty has been replaced with an understanding that you will one day see again that wonderful animal who so filled your life. The dark cloud that hung over you now has a very pronounced silver lining. There is still pain and longing because of his/her absence, but that is normal. But now the longing is fueled by hope and not grief.

I want to end on a very upbeat note. This book contains a number of true accounts of the perseverance and faithfulness of pets, among other stories. The stories were presented in such a way so as to illustrate a point that I was trying to make. There was no ulterior motive, only the hope that they would help.

I think when we share our own stories with each other, it helps. It lets us know that we are not alone, that God or life or fate has not singled us out to suffer and no one else. This in turn helps us to put our situation in proper perspective. Moreover, just reading about some of the accomplishments of our magnificent animal friends is very uplifting.

To that end, I thought it might be appropriate to finish my work with a few more uplifting and humorous stories. The difference would be that I am just sharing them for your amusement, there is no point to be made. Most, but not all of them are taken from my own experiences. I have not embellished upon them in the slightest. I hope they make you smile and warm your heart.

CHAPTER 7
STORIES OF HUMOR

Scooter and the "kitty"

The first dog I ever had was a wonderful animal that cost me all of my 12th year birthday money. Scooter came out of a cardboard box sitting in a department store, marked $4.99. He was perhaps the best bargain of my young life. He was definitely the best investment, for he paid out years of devotion and friendship that my human friends could never give me. He was a great dog, protective and faithful. He never wandered more than 20 feet from me when I and my friends went out playing in the fields that bordered the local river or railroad tracks.

On one of our escapades, Scooter and I were at one of our favorite places, a place that probably accounts for many of the grey hairs on my mother's head. In the woods, across the railroad tracks from our clubhouse was a large marble yard. The marble slabs were huge, as wide as the widest refrigerator and twice as long, weighing several tons. The slabs were stacked 4 or 5 high with railroad ties between the slabs to give the stacks stability.

There were easily hundreds of stacks in about a 2 acre parcel of land. Each stack was different in shape and stability. Some, we learned, would wobble when you jumped on them from another stack, much like the trick stones on some Disney rides.

My club, which consisted of six or seven pre-teen boys and our dogs, used this marble yard to hide and play in, to blow off fireworks, or to climb the stacks to reach the ripest mulberries on the big trees. It was a grand place that we all loved with the same passion our mothers loathed it. Many a fractured skull had come crying home from this enchanting place.

116

CHAPTER 7
STORIES OF HUMOR

On this occasion, only Scooter and I were in the marble yard. I was jumping from stack to stack above, while he chased me from twenty feet below. The fact that I could have fallen and split my head open (again) did nothing to keep us from having the time of our lives.

I made some quick maneuvers, jumping rapidly across 4 stacks of marble, which I felt sure would confuse Scooter, looking up from below. When I laid down on one of the top slabs and peeked over the edge, he was nowhere to be seen and I thought I had fooled him. A moment later I heard him yelping and barking from what seemed to be a great distance away.

I jumped to a lower stack and then about a dozen feet to a pile of soft dirt below and began looking for him, only to find that he hadn't been very far away at all. He had just been barking halfway under one of the bottom slabs, which muffled his bark and gave the impression that he was farther away.

He was aggressively digging and barking under this slab, so I got on my hands and knees to see what he was after. I knew feral cats often had their kittens under the slabs, so it did not surprise me to see the silhouette of a cat back in the dark, under the slab, near to where Scooter was. I egged him on by saying "get him Scooter, get him boy".

Now, before you think me an insensitive wretch or cat hater, please let me explain. Scooter was all bark. He always had been. I knew it and he knew it. He was a very fast dog. He had often chased cats and rabbits through our yard, and usually caught them. And when he did, he would stop, back off and sit there not knowing what he was supposed to do next.

117

He apparently knew that chasing cats was what dogs did, but I guess no one ever explained to him why. His modus operandi was to chase, jump and hold down, then back off and watch them. He never bit them, never growled, never barked (except before the chase). He just seemed to like to chase them. Unfortunately for him, usually when he backed off, the victim cat would give him a quick swipe with their claws before making their escape. Even then, Scooter did nothing.

So, knowing this, I had no reservations egging him on. After doing so, I maneuvered myself to the place I thought the cat would exit when Scooter successfully flushed him out so I could catch him. Before I knew what was happening, the "cat" popped out from the darkness and, right before my eyes, transformed itself into a skunk. And a very angry skunk at that. I had no time to react. Scooter came shooting out of the hole behind the skunk at the same time I was choosing a quick escape route, while trying hard not to get bit by the skunk.

I think I might have made it too, except for Scooter. He jumped on the skunk in his normal way and, to be honest, I don't really remember what happened next, except to say that the immediate area was enveloped in a rather sickening cloud of skunk musk.

The only experience I have ever had that came close to that nauseating day was going through the gas chamber at Navy Recruit Training. But at least a quick shower took the gas residue off. Not so skunk gas. Everything you see in the cartoons is true. Your eyes burn, your skin burns, your face burns and you cannot breathe without gagging.

STORIES OF HUMOR

You have to scrub yourself raw and when you are done doing that, you have to scrub again. Your clothes are permanent casualties and throwing them out is an option, but burying them is a better one. If you have long hair, kiss it goodbye as well. And finally, you must scrub again.

Scooter and I both learned a valuable lesson that day. I cannot speak for Scooter, but I know I never forgot it. There is a big difference between kitties and skunks!

Duke the Dangerous

As was common among career military families back in the 1950's and 60's, money was scarce and so was adequate housing. When your family uprooted because your father was transferred to a new duty station, it was fairly certain that it would be several months before you occupied your own semi-permanent residence again and life returned to normal.

The good thing about military life however, and in particular the Submarine Service that my father was a part of, is that you generally traveled in the company of people you were stationed with before. Usually the entire crew and boat moves at the same time, at least in those days.

There exists camaraderie among sailors and their families that you just don't see in the everyday structure of our society. As shipmates, sailors become almost completely dependent upon each other at sea. Some provide the meals, others the medicine, still others navigate the ship through dangerous waters while you sleep. There is great mutual trust and dependence.

That trust builds during the long, arduous months at sea, and sailors become very close friends. This closeness is carried home to the families, who in turn grow closer to other families as they support each other in the absence of their sailors.

Within the families of men and women who wear dolphins on their uniform (devices that tell all they meet that they are submariners), there exists such a closeness that it is sometimes hard to tell where one family leaves off and another begins. They depend upon each other for childcare, transportation and even lodging when times are tough. Often during the times of family transfer, homes of shipmates are opened to accommodate those in transit and their families. Dogs, cats, goldfish and whatever else comes with the family are welcomed into the homes of shipmates who are already established in a household at the new duty station. It is not an inconvenience to have shipmates staying with you, it is a way of life.

Such was the case in 1959 when my father was reassigned to the Submarine Base in Groton, Connecticut. Housing was hard to get and money was very, very tight. Some wonderful shipmates opened their small home to us for several weeks. Dad, mom, my sister, brother, grandmother, myself and the cat all were welcomed. It was awkward and crowded, but a spirit of "can do" prevailed as shipmate helped shipmate.

While living with these selfless folks, I felt compelled to do whatever I could do to express my family's gratitude. Daily I cleaned and kept the entire house orderly. I cleaned bathrooms, made beds, ran errands and took out the trash. I also volunteered to walk their dog whenever the need arose.

STORIES OF HUMOR

I wanted to make their lives as comfortable as I possibly could to offset the inconvenience of my family's presence in their home. I know I was only a pre-teen and that responsibility was not mine, but I just felt burdened to take the responsibility. But I was not prepared for what walking the dog entailed.

Their dog was a large grayish-brown boxer named Duke. He was everything you would expect a boxer named Duke not to be. When I first heard his name, it conjured up visions of John Wayne and I was prepared for a stately, strong willed stallion of a dog. He was far from living up to that expectation however. He looked like a boxer, with that noble stance that boxers have. He held his head high and looked every bit the centurion of the premises. But looks certainly can be deceiving.

The woman of the house took me on my break-in walk with Duke. She said there were certain "things" I had to do. I did not give much thought to that comment because I knew dogs, and whatever "things" went along with the walk, well I was just the boy to handle it.

She put Duke on a leash and asked me to follow her outside. As we were walking, she explained that Duke had some very chronic ailments that made him sickly and weak. I would find out later that the gentleman of the house, a rugged old sailor, didn't like the dog for exactly the same ailments that I was about to learn about.

We had not gone very far, when the dog began his business. I noted that he had a very profound case of the runs (I wish there were a nicer way to put that). She explained that this was normal for him because of the medication she gave him for his ailments.

When he had completed his business, instead of scratching up the turf as most dogs do, he turned himself backward to the woman and (I know you won't believe this, but it is true), she took a handful of tissues from her pocket and wiped the dog!

I was shocked. At my tender age I had never seen anything quite so shocking. I looked around to see if anyone was watching. I was embarrassed. No one wipes a dog for goodness sake. I fought back the urge to tell her that perhaps I had been too hasty in offering to walk her dog. Instead, when she asked if I had any reservations in performing this job, I politely answered "no ma'am".

I was lying. I had a BIG problem. I did my job for a couple of days. I treated the dog as if he was an invalid. I wiped him. I hated every moment of it, but I wiped him. Eventually, I came to my wit's end. I had performed my last wipe and I was not going to wipe again. This dog was pitiful and I was going to make a man out of him, so to speak.

I began by walking him near the garden hose. When he needed wiping, he got washed. He didn't like that very much, but there wasn't much he could do. Then, to dry him off, I made him run. I actually had to teach him how to run. It was like a light went on in his head..."you mean I can run"? He ran and jumped as if he had just been let out of prison. He was excited and from somewhere deep inside a flood of energy erupted from that dog. We went from my dragging him, to his running alongside, to his dragging me.

STORIES OF HUMOR

I was getting so worn out keeping up with him that I decided to take him off the leash. My goodness, it was like he turned into super dog. He ran around the courtyard of the apartments at a lightning pace, greeting everyone he encountered with a wagging of that stubby little tail that boxers have. I swear when he greeted them, he smiled and I knew it was his way of telling everyone "look at me, look at me, I am alive". He stayed only a second before heading to the next person. It was like his coming out party and he was taking his bows.

He came back to me in a sweat each and every time and we would re-leash and walk back to his house. He was so much more lively and energetic now. Coincidentally, as soon as his running started, his runs stopped.

The second week, I took Duke to a pond down in the cow pasture behind the apartment complex. We chased frogs and snakes and even fish. He learned how to enjoy mud and water, the way boys were supposed to. We went to the pond every day after that. It was the high time of our day. I would have to wash him with the garden hose and dry him off before we got home or the pond smell would surely give us away.

One day at the pond, the cows moved in to water. They were everywhere, perhaps 40 or 50 of them. They walked right up on us and bullied us out of the way. They were making it clear to us that the pond belonged to them and they wanted us to move. We just wanted our little part of the pond, but when we tried to go there, the cows would turn and face us as if they were prepared to defend it from our intrusion. They may have been bluffing, but I wasn't going to push it.

One of the cows made a half-hearted move toward us to scare us off and Duke growled. I had never heard him growl before. This gave me an idea. I pointed at the cows and said "sic em Duke". I wasn't expecting much reaction, but to my surprise Duke took off barking and charging the cows like he had been doing it all his life.

The cows apparently were as surprised as I, reacting in concert to this unexpected aggression, fleeing no doubt for what they thought was their lives. Duke was unbelievable. He had that pond cleared of cows in less than 30 seconds. The whole herd was on the run. I was dumbfounded. I had made a monster out of the dog. And I was glad. In fact, I was proud. Duke had graduated. He was a real dog now. And he knew it too. He came back with his chest puffed out and a different air about him. And it wasn't just the swamp algae hanging from his face that made him look tough. He had arrived!

Now when I walked Duke, he pulled me on the leash and walked proudly. He barked at every other dog he saw as if to say "you aren't going to laugh at me anymore".

No one back at the house knew what Duke and I had been up to. I went to great pains to keep Duke under control and looking like his old self while in the house. It went rather well, until a knock came on the door one evening.

Duke heard the knock and went absolutely ballistic, barking and jumping and carrying on. This was something he had learned all on his own. Perhaps it is just something dogs naturally do. Whatever the reason, it took me as much by surprise as it did everyone else.

CHAPTER 7
STORIES OF HUMOR

When he charged the door and made such a fuss, I thought for sure the woman of the house was going to have a heart attack. She clutched her chest and just stood there speechless. The only way I can describe it is to say she had a look of terror on her face. Something bad had happened to her Duke and she was visibly shaken.

She focused her eyes on me and it appeared she had almost instantaneously figured out that I was the cause for this awful display she was seeing in Duke. I was sure she was about to say something, when to my relief, her husband jumped out of his easy chair and said "what on earth has come over that dog"? And then, reaching down to Duke on the back, he added "good boy, good boy".

To be honest, I don't remember if the door was ever answered. It probably was, but I don't remember. I was too busy holding my breath to see what kind of trouble I was in. When the smoke had cleared (Duke settled down), the husband wanted to know what had happened to Duke. He was apparently very pleased with the dog that now stood before him.

I explained in detail what we had been up to, leaving out anything that I thought would get me in trouble, such as chasing the cows. I told them of the running and the pond. I told them the diarrhea had stopped. I told them that even the other dogs in the neighborhood now gave Duke space.

The woman was horrified. She cried. But the man laughed out loud and thanked me. He patted me on the back and said "things are going to be different around here for me and Duke".

CHAPTER 7
STORIES OF HUMOR

Fuji and the Bug

We had a solid black Siamese cat named Fuji (pictured on the cover), who was quite the character. By necessity, he was an outdoor cat and that suited him just fine. He was a tough guy tom and liked to roam, quarrel with other toms and just cause general unrest with the other neighborhood cats.

He also enjoyed the woods where we lived in Connecticut. He became very familiar with his surroundings and very comfortable as well. He would go out hunting into the woods and bring us little presents from the woods, which I will not discuss in detail here. Cat people know what I mean.

Somewhere near his third birthday, we were reassigned to the city of Miami. We packed up and moved and quickly settled into our new home there. Fuji had no trouble making the physical adjustment to the more tropical environment. It was a bit hotter and more humid, but he seemed to adjust very well. But there were dangerous differences that neither of us had anticipated.

One morning, I saw him playing with what looked like a large insect. He often did this, so I was not too concerned. He caught cockroaches and those large palmetto bugs and toyed with them until he tired of it, as cats are inclined to do. Something about this insect seemed different however, and I moved closer to get a better look. I immediately recognized the creature he held in his paws as a scorpion. As a child I had lived in Key West and had many experiences with them, including a scorpion farm I used to keep in the outside shed, until my mother discovered it. I can still hear her screaming.

126

Fuji was swatting the insect back and forth like a hockey puck and the critter was becoming very agitated. Having been stung myself, I knew the wallop their sting carries, so I moved as quickly as I could to try to stop the inevitable. Had I thought my action out a bit more, I probably would have opted to approach Fuji more slowly and soothingly. Instead, I hurried my movement and that caused him to think I was attempting to steal his new found "toy". He pounced on the scorpion, picking it up in his mouth to run off. The now angry scorpion thrust his weapon, but somehow missed Fuji's face, sinking his stinger deep into his upper shoulder.

Fuji did at least a triple somersault with a one and a half twist, landed on all fours, and began wailing like only a Siamese can. He sounded just like a baby crying, but with an unearthly twang to it. Then, he headed straight up the nearest scrub pine.

If you are not familiar with scrub pines, they are unique trees in that they have no branches until you are about to the top of the tree. They grow almost perfectly straight and top out at about 50 or 60 feet. The branches start at about 40 to 45 feet. Fuji went strait up the tree without stopping until he reached the upper branches about 50 from the ground.

I was very upset because I knew he could die if he had received too much venom. A person who does not have an allergy to the venom can take a sting and it is not much worse than a wasp, but a smaller animal can be overwhelmed by the toxin. I wanted to get him to a veterinarian as soon as possible, but there was just no way of getting him down. Climbing the tree would require a primate. Cutting it down would pose a greater risk to his life. And the fire department would not come.

So we waited. And we waited. We called out to him and tried to coax him down, but he would not come. So we waited. And we waited. That stubborn cat sat in that tree all day and into the night. I checked on him several times during the night and he was still up there. In the morning I tried again, but he would not move. I concentrated hard to see if I could detect movement. I was afraid he had passed away on the branch. But every so often he would wag his tail.

For 3 days and nights he sat in that tree. Eventually he turned his head and looked down at us when we called up to him, but he would not move. By this time I realized he was out of danger from the venom, but now I was worried about him not ever coming down. Finally, on the fourth day, we heard him crying at the door. I quickly grabbed him and hugged him and gave him the once over. His arm was still swollen, so swollen in fact, that he looked like he had been pumping weights. It was puffed up to make him look like the feline Charles Atlas.

He made a full recovery and became his same old self. I never saw him playing with bugs again though. And somehow I think he missed Connecticut.

Miko's swan song

It is my opinion that some of the best animals you can come by are those without pedigree. I am not putting down those animals that have them, only underscoring the potential of those that do not. We acquired a "mutt" in the conventional sense of the word. She was a mixture of so many breeds, we stopped counting.

STORIES OF HUMOR

But that was not a detriment in anyway. She was one of the most intelligent and energetic dogs that we ever shared our lives with. Her name was Miko and she was an extraordinary animal.

And she loved to swim. Her first introduction to water was at my mother's house in New Jersey. Mom had a pool with a wooden platform surrounding it. While I was swimming one day, Miko came up the ladder to see what I was doing. I coaxed her into the water over my mother's protests. At first she sort of inched her way over the edge to see what it felt like, but in one quick movement, she jumped right in. The jump was similar to that of a Jack Russell Terrier. Perhaps that was one of her many mixes.

She swam to me, then around the pool awhile, splashing with her paws as she doggy-paddled, trying to catch the water her paws splashed up at the same time. I showed her where the stairs were and she climbed right out. I thought she was through, but she went back to the place she had first entered the pool and jumped right in again. She did not even stop to shake herself off as dogs usually do.

She continued jumping in, swimming to the ladder, running back to the entry point and jumping in again. I tired of the water and wanted her to stop. The problem was, she did not want to get out. She had found something she really liked to do and she wasn't about to give it up. She was a water junky! So, employing my superior intellect, I put her back down on the ground and removed the only ladder leading to the platform. She went through some minor withdrawal pains, but she survived.

No too long after this, we were back home in Connecticut walking Miko in a small park. There was no one else around, so we decided to take her off her leash and let her run. We had forgotten her addiction to water. Wouldn't you know that she headed straight for the little pond in the corner of the park.

She stopped and looked at the water for a moment, as if she was wondering why it had no platform and was bigger than the pool she remembered. Then, before I could react, she picked out a huge boulder on the shore that extended out into the water, jumped up on the rock and plunged right in. She then swam ashore, ran back to the rock and jumped right in again. She had not forgotten her experience at mom's.

None of us had noticed a big white swan swimming nearby. The swan was apparently coming over to see what all the commotion was about. For those of you who are not familiar with the habits of swans, they are very territorial. Their looks are very deceiving...they make formidable aggressors. Miko had not seen the swan at first, but as it moved closer to the rock, the movement caught her attention. Miko looked hesitatingly at the bird, then back at me, then back at the bird, and then jumped in and started after it.

She reached the swan in pretty good time, but I do not think the encounter went quite as Miko expected. The crafty swan had slowly inched further out into the pond, allowing Miko to reach it only when it was sure it had the advantage. It was not afraid of the dog, only stacking the deck in its favor. Miko barked wildly as she swam and I could tell that she was tiring because her bark was labored. I was sure that I would have to dive in and rescue her soon.

CHAPTER 7
STORIES OF HUMOR

The swan waited patiently for Miko to be far enough from shore that she could not easily escape and then it made its move. It swam quickly to my dog, so quick that it startled Miko. I am sure in her mind she was thinking "hey, things I chase aren't supposed to chase me". It was obvious to me that it was obvious to Miko that she had misjudged the situation. The bird was a lot bigger close up...and not at all like those pigeons she chased earlier.

The bird started pecking at her head and buffeting her with its large wings. She was trying to push Miko's head under the water and drown her. I heard Miko yelp out loudly as she turned to flee to shore. It was clear that she was willing to forget the whole matter...she would leave the pond if the darn bird would just leave her alone. But it wouldn't.

That swan beat Miko up pretty badly, biting and pecking on the almost defenseless dog all the way to the shore. She made Miko swallow enough water to satisfy her need to jump in that pond ever again.

I was happy that I did not have to go in to rescue her, but a little angry at myself for letting the situation get out of my control. As she climbed out of the water with her tail between her legs, I thought maybe this had been for the best. Miko had made it to shore a little worse for the wear, but a whole lot wiser in the things of the world. She would never make that mistake again. In fact, on subsequent walks to that park, she would not venture near that pond. There were too many swans there to know which one it was that took Miko to school, but I am sure whichever one it was puffed out its chest feathers a little bit more each time Miko walked by.

STORIES OF HUMOR

Samantha and the Mystery Dog

While stationed in Miami, my family and I occasionally enjoyed taking a small boat out fishing in the mud flats of the Florida Bay off the Florida Keys. One particular area that I favored was just south of Marathon Key, a little northwest of the famous 7 mile bridge that exits Marathon heading south to Key West. There is a string of mangrove islands offshore in that area that seem to be popular with the local fish population. I have caught Bonefish, Tarpon, Barracuda, Sharks, Snappers and a host of other fish in these areas.

On one of our trips, it was exceedingly more hot than usual. The wind was calm and it was summer. You know the old question "is it hotter in the summer or in Miami"? The answer is "Miami". We had a bimini top, which protected us from the sun above, but the glare from the water negated the effects shade usually has.

We had been swimming in the flats. I loved to swim when the water looked like glass and it was between tides. There is no need to anchor the boat during such times for there is absolutely no wind or water movement. The water is like a large window to a beautiful world of color and life.

We were in the boat eating lunch, sitting motionless a few dozen yards from an atoll shaped mangrove island. It was hot, but still very enjoyable. My wife and children sat eating and drinking cold sodas, contemplating where we would motor to next, while I alone braved the sizzling sun and stood on the bow searching for fish or conch shells. Apparently, they too had sought the shade, for there were none to be seen.

CHAPTER 7
STORIES OF HUMOR

To be fair, I wasn't the only one who was braving the sun. My trusted West Highland White Terrier, Samantha (pictured on the cover), was in her normal position, standing right next to me. She was panting and very uncomfortable because of her thick coat. Thankfully, it was white and did not absorb as much heat as it would if it were darker. Nevertheless, she was obviously hot. But nothing I could say would make her leave my side.

As she stood on her hind legs with her front paws on the railing of the boat, one of the many large birds in the mangrove trees on the island moved and the movement caught her attention. Because from our distance the white birds looked more like blossoms on the green mangrove branches, she wasn't sure what she had seen. But ever the vigilant guard, she felt she had to give at least a cursory, half-hearted bark.

The mangrove trees were so thick that they immediately bounced the sound back toward the boat. The echo of her bark startled her. She apparently thought that there was a dog on the island. She quickly jumped up on the railing and let out a more emphatic bark, which in short order came back to her more emphatically. By now, Samantha's hair was standing up on her back and she was agitated. She was barking rapidly now and because echoes do not wait, they too came back rapidly.

Well, the whole thing was getting out of hand. Samantha was now running up and down the rail of the boat barking feverishly. She looked like she was going to jump in and swim to the island. My family and I were laughing so hard at the whole spectacle that we probably could have done nothing to prevent her. And I really did not want to go to the island to get her because in the depths of the mangroves lives hordes of hungry mosquitoes.

133

Somehow Samantha managed to restrain herself from jumping in, and my wife and I regained our composure enough to get her down from the side rail. She wouldn't let it go, however. As we motored away to another island, she jumped up on the bow and continued to bark. Only when we were far enough away that there was no longer an echo did she stop. I am sure that in Sam's mind, she was the victor, having chased off that mysterious intruder.

The Horses of Guantanamo Bay

During my years in the Navy, as I think any sea-going sailor can claim, our ship made several trips to Guantanamo Bay, Cuba, more affectionately known as GTMO (pronounced gitmo). Here ships and crews undergo extensive testing for seaworthiness and proficiency, usually on an annual basis.

During one of these periods, I was given the day off for having worked so hard at my job. At least that is what they told me. So, I was to spend the day ashore while my aircraft carrier left port without me. This was very unusual, but since I seldom took advantage of liberty in ports away from home, I decided it might be fun.

Thinking back now, I still wonder why this unusual and unique opportunity was extended to me. Usually you get foul-ups off the ship during important inspections. I was not a "foul-up". In fact, I received many accolades for my contributions and leadership. I was an important member of the operations division and it just didn't make sense that they were sailing without me. At the time it did not bother me, but now, many years later, somehow it does. It just doesn't make sense.

CHAPTER 7
STORIES OF HUMOR

Could it be that they just did not want the inspectors to see me? I think that was it. The inspectors were the same people from the previous year and we had had a rather memorable moment during their last visit. I had inadvertently, and quite innocently, injured the Chief Inspector, a Captain (O-6 in the Navy) whose name now escapes me.

What happened was really just a fluke. The good Captain wanted to check certain operational files to ensure that we were keeping them as prescribed. As he announced his desire, he stepped forward positioning himself directly in front of the filing cabinets. As he stepped forward, he also pointed at the bottom drawer of the cabinet. Naturally, I thought this was the drawer he wanted opened, so I jumped to it rather smartly and pulled open the sliding drawer.

Apparently, he was one of those individuals who needs to use their fingers to read and what I perceived as his selecting the bottom drawer was in fact, just his pointing at the drawer to read the label. As I turned to open the drawer, I had no way of knowing that he had quickly scanned the other drawer labels and decided he wanted to look in the top drawer. As you might imagine, as he stepped to retrieve the top drawer, I flung the bottom drawer open in smart military fashion.

The Chief Inspector did a very good job of controlling the volume of his expressed agony, but little could be done to keep his dignity after a bonehead stunt like that. Everyone in the room had witnessed what had happened. I had responded as any good sailor would. I knew it. The Chief Inspector knew it. Everyone knew it.

He grimaced a bit longer and rubbed his ankle, but said nothing about the incident. He then completed his task and left. He was very gracious about the whole thing. Unfortunately, it still came up in our critique of the trials and I caught a few "ribbings" about it. I think one of the comments was "Hey Gary, I heard you know how to 'drawer' out the best in Captains".

So, if my absence from the ship was by design, it was to keep from reminding the inspectors of the previous year's fiasco. Still, I doubt that was the reason, because several sailors from other ships had also been let off for the day and those I spoke with said that they too had been selected for a day off as a reward for their good work. Could it be that I was not alone in my history of inspector assault, or had the Admiral really decided to give a day off to one person on each ship for outstanding work? I suppose I will never know, but I prefer to believe the latter.

That was not the humorous story I wanted to tell. That was only the background for setting the story up. Once on the island, several of the men from the other ships and I ran into each other at one of the few attractions on the base, the livery stables. Here you could rent a horse for an hour tour around an established trail.

The stables contained about a dozen horses, all of which were reported to give quiet, soothing rides around the marked course. I thought this would be a good diversion. More importantly, it was cheap. The horses were good looking creatures, well fed and well padded. They reacted very well to petting and appeared friendly enough. So, we paid our money and chose our animals. We then departed on a journey I have never forgotten.

CHAPTER 7
STORIES OF HUMOR

I cannot say for sure how long the course was, but certainly it was not very long, perhaps between one-quarter and one-half mile. We started out with the horses walking at a slow pace and then picked it up to a faster walk. We hadn't gotten 200 feet from the barn however, when the horses came to a grinding halt. Not one of them, but all of them...almost as if by command.

We encouraged them repeatedly to move forward and after about 20 minutes of doing so, had only gained about the same amount of footage. A foot a minute seemed to be a little unsatisfactory to me. The trail was clearly marked and well-traveled and I could not understand why my horse did not want to go. I dismounted and pulled on the reigns, dragging him along. The horse actually pulled back on me in rebellion and gave me that white-eyed look horses give when they don't agree with you.

Having some experience with horses, I decided to show him who was boss and I bullied him along for another hundred feet or more, until I tired. I did not hurt the animal. I only took charge and let him know that I was as stubborn as he. The other fellows were having similar problems, but they were far behind me now and I really lost interest in anything else around me. My whole being, my whole purpose, was to ride this horse. It was me and this stubborn, unreasonable animal, alone in the world, locked in a battle of the wills.

I tried everything. I was kind. I spoke sweet nothings in his ear. I bribed him. I pulled grasses up for him to eat. Nothing. I changed tactics. I yelled. I screamed. I cried. I tried embarrassing him. I told him he was shameful. Nothing worked. Nothing but pulling.

And so I pulled, and pulled, and pulled, for the next 45 minutes. Inch by inch we made our way out, around and back on that trail. By the time I had gotten to where I could see the barn again through the trees, I was a soiled sweating mess. I had human sweat on top of horse sweat on top of dirt from pulling up grass. I was disheveled and dirty and I smelled like a horse. I was worn out and tapped of all energy. But he was moving! And that was what this was all about after all. I was winning! Wasn't I?

I don't know where the marker was, but somewhere after we cleared the trees and we could see the barn clearly, that horse suddenly came to life and took off like a bolt of lightning. He didn't warn me. He didn't even give me a hint. He saw his stable and that was that. He jerked me clear off the ground and dragged me down the remainder of the path. I had never understood that term "he smelled the barn" until I actually saw it in action.

I was not only exhausted, but now I was humiliated. And as I tried to dust off the humility with the dirt, the stable hand asked "Did you have a good ride?" He knew I hadn't. He knew no one ever did. He was in cahoots with the horses. Together their job was to take money from sailors and then strip them of their dignity.

No doubt he had heard me bragging earlier that I had been on horses before and learned from the Blackfoot Nation how to handle them. No doubt he knew just what scam artists those horses were. And no doubt he wanted to teach me a lesson. But I wasn't going to give him the satisfaction. Sore and worn, sweaty and smelly, I mustered whatever pride I had left and answered him "oh it was the best, thanks".

CHAPTER 7
STORIES OF HUMOR

"Bear"ing it all at the Coast Guard Academy

During one of my tours in the United States Coast Guard, I was assigned to the staff of the Superintendent, U. S. Coast Guard Academy in New London, Connecticut. I was the senior member of the Academy Special Security Force. My duties included supervising 20 other security personnel in special functions that demanded crowd control, parking assistance, automobile searches, funeral details and other undesirable duties that our regular security force didn't feel like doing.

One morning in 1981 I received a telephone call ordering me to organize my special security force for a special assignment. I notified my force and told everyone to arrive in Service Dress Blues, the uniform of the day, with full security gear and helmets.

When I arrived, I asked the Officer of the Day what the special assignment was and was told that the Academy mascot, a 100 pound northern black bear, had escaped from her pen. He was creating havoc in the community surrounding the Academy, i.e. turning over trash cans, scaring children and dogs, etc. My job was to recapture the mascot. Needless to say, no one was happy that we were going to have to accomplish this task in our dress uniform, myself included...but we had no time to change.

Knowing that bears usually return to their den after rummaging, I figured he would come back to the Academy grounds and his cage. It was the only place familiar to him. I posted people at strategic locations believing they would be there for a very long time waiting on the bear. To my surprise, within fifteen minutes the bear was spotted back on campus. We organized ourselves by radio and converged on that location.

The bear immediately figured out what our intentions were and broke for the football field, probably the area best known by a campus mascot. Once there, he made fools of us, running in and out of bleachers, around the press box and finally under the bleachers.

I was not sure what to do at this juncture as there was not much more than crawl space under that section of bleachers and it was very dark and very wet. About the same time, a good friend of mine, the only force member I was not able to locate, came walking out of the enlisted club. He had obviously been drinking (he was off duty) and was "feeling good", if you know what I mean.

He asked "what's going on Gary"? I explained what was going on and then added "But we have it under control, why don't you just go sleep it off"? I returned to the problem at hand and forgot about my friend, thinking he would follow my advice. I don't know how he managed it, but before I knew what was going on, he managed to crawl under the bleachers and was crawling toward the bear.

I kneeled down and tried to see back up in the dark shadows of the bleachers, but I was not able to discern any of the shapes I saw. I was able to hear however. My inebriated friend had apparently not located the bear yet, for he was calling loudly "Here kitty kitty kitty". The entire security force broke out in hysterical laughter at this drunken display of bravado. We were in stitches and in danger of losing all objectivity, when we were brought back to reality by a loud growl and my friend's scream. We learned later that he had found the bear, grabbed its stub tail and the bear had retaliated with a quick bite on the hand.

140

Almost simultaneously with the scream, that rascal bear came darting out from under the bleachers, heading for the lower football field. His way was blocked however, as we had anticipated he might bolt and had surrounded the immediate area. As soon as he realized that he was surrounded by officers, he scurried up the nearest tree. And as you might guess, it was not one of the smaller ones that he could have chosen.

A few moments later the state Fish and Game Commission agents I had summoned earlier in case we needed to tranquilize the bear, arrived on scene. To my chagrin, they did not come with the tranquilizing equipment, explaining that they did not have access to it on the weekends. I wondered out loud, but under my breath why they had come at all. But they wanted to help and I welcomed their expertise in capturing wild aimals.

That welcome was short-lived. Their first (and only) plan was one I did not support or condone. Briefly, they wanted someone to climb up the tree and tie a rope off at about 20 feet below the 50 foot mark where the bear had decided to sit. The idea was to tie the rope to their truck and shake the tree back and forth, scaring the bear into coming down. I protested, but they assured me this was a tactic that always worked. So I temporarily turned the mission over to them. One of them climbed up and tied off the rope on the tree. Then they tied the rope to the bumper of the truck. They began their plan of rocking the tree back and forth. A short lunge of the truck forward, then throwing the transmission into neutral and being pulled back a bit, then again in drive. The tree shook and, amazingly, the bear actually did begin to stir. In fact, he moved down the tree a foot or two. A few more shakes and the bear was on his way down. He definitely did not like the tree shaking.

When he reached the 35 foot mark, he decided to head back up the tree. The men from the state over-reacted to this change of plans and hit the gas a little too hard. The tree bent to the point of almost breaking, but the rope gave way first.

The tree, now free from the rope's tautness, was transformed into a catapult. That poor bear was thrown some 15 feet through the air and 40 feet down. I cringed. I thought the little guy was history. To my amazement, he hit the ground on all fours, never missing a step, and he was off to the races.

He was past me before I realized that he had weathered the fall. I started off right behind him, in full dress uniform with my utility belt, handcuffs and billy club flopping all around. My helmet was bouncing around on my head, giving me the appearance of the head on one of those hula girl dolls people put on the dashboards of their cars. Lumbering down the trail through a small patch of woods, I chased after that bear all the way down to the softball and soccer fields of the lower campus.

I was surprised at the speed of this small creature. He was less than 24 inches high on all fours, but his feet seemed to never touch the ground. I knew bears were fast, but I never suspected they were able to put on bursts of speed like this little guy was. I was right behind him though, shedding my cumbersome gear and jacket as I ran. I thought by lightening my load I would be able to catch up to him, but that proved to be yet another miscalculation on my part. Despite my speed increase, he managed to keep the same distance between us.

He arrived at the lower field ahead of me, but rather than entering the field, he turned south on the railroad tracks that transit the lower campus. This was a break for me because the spaces between the railroad ties proved a hindrance to him. So I poured it on and finally managed to pull along side of him.

I threw all my weight into him trying to knock him off the track and getting him to roll. It had little effect, except that I lost some ground. I again came along side him and this time tackled him. We both rolled off the tracks and onto the shoulder of the track mound. I recovered from the roll faster than he and I pounced on his back. I knew that as a 200 pound weightlifter, I would be able to control this smaller 100 pound youngster.

This was yet another miscalculation. He got up on all fours with me square on his back and my arms around his neck, and started running toward the adjacent cyclone fence. I could not believe the power of this small animal. About this time, four other men arrived and jumped on my back. They had been laboring to catch up to us carrying a large volleyball net they thought might come in handy. Before jumping on my back, they threw this net over the bear and me.

We had him now, or so we thought. That stubborn bear continued moving toward the fence with all five of us on his back. We must have presented at least half a ton of weight, yet he was able to stand and move. He dragged us about a dozen more feet and was finally stopped only because he tried to climb under the fence and got his head stuck. Otherwise, I am not sure we would have held him.

We took advantage of the situation. While he struggled with the fence, we began wrapping the net around him to contain him. Someone thought to bring the Academy ambulance on scene. It probably was brought in the event someone needed to be treated, but as it turned out, we used it to transport the bear.

I know it sounds ridiculous, but the now 20 people on scene could not handle that little fireball of a bear. I made the decision to take everything, the bear, the net and me and throw us in the back of the ambulance and ferry us over to the bear's large cage. Somehow, as this tangled mass was lifted into the ambulance, I was fortunate enough to slide out just before the doors were slammed shut.

It actually proved to be the easiest part of the entire event. Everything went relatively smooth, considering what we had previously gone through, and we all finally had a chance to relax. Our guard was let down too prematurely however, as no sooner had the doors on the ambulance closed, than the bear commenced a terrible ruckus inside.

He was obviously trying to get himself out of the net too. He thrashed around inside the ambulance, knocking over equipment and ripping things off the inner bulkheads. We learned later that he had bit holes in the cushions of the portable personnel carriers, among other things, and left deep scratch marks in the floor surface, presumably from trying to dig his way out. When we eventually opened the doors, we were stunned at what damage he had done inside. How could one little bear cause so much trouble?

STORIES OF HUMOR

We backed the ambulance right up to the edge of his cage. In the event he somehow broke our grip on him when we opened the ambulance, I wanted him to have no opportunity to go anywhere but into his cage.

This bear was not through surprising us however. Now, with ambulance doors wide open, he decides that the ambulance he fought so hard to get out of wasn't that bad after all and he refused to leave. He backed up into a corner and started growling and snapping at our attempts to pull him out. He also tried to take swipes at us with his filed down claws, but because the net was still wrapped around his upper torso, his range was hampered.

I know I will sound as if I am embellishing a bit, but that 100 pound bear fought off all our attempts to pull him out for about 20 minutes. Finally, in frustration, I mustered up my courage, jumped up in the ambulance, gathered up as much of the net as I could, flung it on top of him and bear-hugged (if you will pardon the pun) the whole pile of net and bear. I quickly lifted the 150 pound bundle as I simultaneously turned toward the fence and half tossed, half carried everything over it, into his cage.

Almost everything went well. We (the bear and I) cleared the ambulance, the dangling portions of net did not get hung up on anything, I muscled everything over the fence without too much effort, BUT, as I did so, that rascal somehow reached through the net and sunk his ¾ inch canines right into my rump. It hurt! It hurt a lot! There wasn't much damage to my pants - just a few puncture marks and a little blood, but the "pinch" of it stung badly.

STORIES OF HUMOR

After dropping the mesh of bear and net over the fence and doing a little dance while rubbing the sting out of my posterior, I jumped the fence to untangle the bear. When he completely emerged from the net, he had this stupid grin on his face, almost a smile. He leaned over, licked my hand and then ran to his water bowl for a drink as if nothing had happened. It was as if he was saying "hey, that was fun, let's do it again sometime".

The last I had heard was that the bear had grown to over 300 pounds. I was very thankful that I was no longer at that station.

ADDENDUM

I have had so many inquiries concerning another portion of scripture, that I felt compelled to address it in the 2nd edition of this book. The easiest way to accomplish this was to add this addendum, which is not actually an addendum, but rather an addition. Still, because it is a change to the book, I felt labeling it an addendum was more appropriate.

In the 8th chapter of Romans, beginning with verse 18, reference made to the suffering of God's "creature" and travailing of his "creation". I receive much mail from people who read this portion of scripture and jump to the conclusion it is speaking of animals. I have been challenged to explain why I do not allude to this portion of scripture to help make my case for animal afterlife. The reason is quite simple. These passages do not address animals, at least not in the way that some suppose.

Verse 22 is making passive, general reference to the entire creation, which includes everything God created, living or inanimate. Truly, the entire creation suffers and travails in pain because of the fall the Garden of Eden. Before the fall, everything was perfect. After, erally everything was changed for the worse. Imperfection abounds and all the woes we have today are a result of that fall. So, in that sense, the whole of creation suffers jointly, including animals.

In the other verses in this portion of scripture, specific reference made to the "creature". This entity spoken of is not the animal. Verse 20 clearly disqualifies animals as it can only apply to people. Moreover, remember the rules of exegesis. We must take what is said the Apostle Paul in context. If you read the entire chapter, the topic ing discussed has absolutely nothing to do with animals, but addresses rather the conflict of our spirit with our flesh (or carnal mind) and what God's thoughts are on this topic.

ADDENDUM

In verse 1, it says "There is therefore" - and when you see the word "therefore", you must go back to see what it is there for! There particularly in verses 15 through 24 of chapter 7, Paul summarizes the ills we have in our weak flesh. He laments over the wickedness of h flesh and how he desires to be more spiritual in nature.

Other names that are used to refer to the flesh Paul speaks of are "the old nature", "the old man" and others that stem from the sam word used for "creature". The "creature" therefore, is clearly the "ol man" or "old nature" of humans - that part of man that need regeneration through the cross of Jesus. In fact, the entire chapte taken in context, speaks to this, not about animals.

Some will still be hung up on the thought they have that "creature" can only be used to refer to animals. That is not so in the context. In Colossians 1:15, we have a reference to Jesus being calle **"the firstborn of every creature"**. Surely Jesus was not an animal Then in verse 23 of that same chapter, we see the gospel wa **"preached to every creature",** and we know the good news delivered only to those who need redemption; people, not animals.

In II Corinthians 5:17 it says **"Therefore, if any man be i Christ, he is a new creature..."**. In Galatians 6:15, it states **"For i Christ Jesus neither circumcision availeth any thing, ne uncircumcision, but a new creature".**

I am sorry that I must burst the bubble of those relying on thes verses to prove that animals have eternal life, but it simply is not sayin this. Animals are hardly discussed, except to be lumped in as part c the creation. The real issue is the "creature" man and the contra between his unregenerate and regenerate selves.

Irrespective of that, no one reading this book should have any ubt but that there is overwhelming evidence that God does have an ernal plan for all animals. I think I have provided sufficient evidence this claim to calm any fears or doubts you might have. The evidence overwhelming already, without having to make Romans chapter 8 y something that it does not.

Just in case there remains even the slightest skepticism in you garding the conclusions I have drawn, I have saved this final passage r you to consider. We have seen it earlier in this book, but I waited ntil now to add irrefutable application where it concerns animals. I pe this thrills you and comforts you as only the Word of God can.

The verse in the spotlight is **Job 12:10**, which I suggest you ad in context of the entire chapter to ensure my application is correct nd it is). Specifically, this verse says: **"In whose hand is the soul of very living thing".**

As we have before ascertained, there are many, even those we ok to as spiritual leaders, who hold to the view that animals are for is world only, that they do not possess souls, and when they pass, that the end of the road for them. They have no souls and they are reatures for this life only.

I find this view to be both presumptuous and theologically nmature. Presumptuous, because the Bible is clear that God valued e creatures he formed with his own hands and called them "very ood", indicating that their existence pleased him. In Revelation 4:11 nd several other passages we are told that God created all things for is own pleasure. The Bible gives record that God, motivated by this leasure and his love, personally and purposely protects and provides r his creatures from Eden past through Millennium future.

149

ADDENDUM

Indeed, his original plan in Eden was that animals (like human) would live forever. God Almighty is the only true constant in all the universe. Everything else, despite what you may think, either change or is subject to change. God is not. He never changes. His immutability is a constant and precludes variance from the Eden plan irrespective of the temporary setback caused by the fall of mankind. is presumptuous to think that God would change his mind on the matter, for his thoughts and plans are perfect and never in need of correction, update or change.

Continuing, I find the idea that animals have no soul theologically immature and lacking. The evidence found in scripture specifically supports that animals do indeed have souls just like people but unlike people, they do not need regeneration. It seems many ministers are content to accept (and ignorantly pass on to others) what they heard from their Seminary Professor rather than study the topic out for themselves.

This voids both their credibility and position, because God warns us to "search out a thing whether it be so" and to "study to show thyself approved...". A shortcut around God's method of "knowing thing" will often lead one to an erroneous view. Such is the case with animals and the question of whether they are eternal or temporal creatures. Job 12:10 gives us specific insight on this topic and trumps and personal ideas, regardless of their academic credentials.

The word "soul" is used in over twenty different ways in the Bible. Invariably, when people come across this word in scripture, they automatically associate it with redemption, so much so that in no matter what context it is used, the connection to salvation is always present in their minds and applied to the interpretation. In most cases, this is right and acceptable, but there are times when it is not.

Clearly, the gospel message is not for animals. I would never suggest otherwise. It is exclusively for people. It is a reconciliatory outreach from God to those in need of salvation. It is not for animals. It is not for angels. The gospel and God's redemption exists for people and people alone. I might add here that it is for all people, that according to scripture, "all have sinned and come short of the Glory of God" (Romans 3:23). Not all will accept God, but it is extended to all.

That said, let me add that while God's redemptive efforts are not directed toward animals, to allow this truth to cause one to draw the conclusion that animals therefore cannot have souls, is to visit a gross injustice on scripture. In fact, the Hebrew word "nephesh" (soul), appears many times in scripture and is used interchangeably to describe both the essence of man and animals. It does not make a distinction between the two and it does not delve into salvation in its application. Rather, it addresses the consciousness of the soul.

This passage in Job is a good example of this point. The word soul is not used in relation to redemption, but rather addresses providential care. A better rendering of its meaning in this verse would be "the life or essence of every living thing...". God is speaking of that part of people and animals that contains or houses the "life" he has given or "breathed" into them.

When we mesh this thought in Job with Romans chapter 8 and Revelation 5:9-13, the meaning is clear, the life or essence of every living thing is in the hand of God. Undoubtedly this means that they are eternally provided for and protected, because there is no more secure place to be than in the almighty and eternally immutable hands of God.

151

ADDENDUM

However, this word in Job indicates an even deeper thought f
us to consider. We often think of ourselves as a flesh and blood bo
with a soul, but in truth, in keeping with the absolute intent of th
word, people are souls that have been placed in flesh and blood bodi
The distinction is subtle, but it is immense in importance and effe
This is our essence, that we are a soul, not a body. The body
temporal, but the soul eternal.

This truth applies to animals as well...they are not creatur
with souls, but are eternal souls (or essences) given temporary bodie
The difference is, unlike humans, and much like the angels, anima
need no redemption. So when we refer to their souls, we are mere
acknowledging that they have essence and that this essence is eternal
nature, not that they are in need of redemption like humans. They a
innocent creatures whose souls are safe in the hand of their creator.

The overwhelming evidence is that the soul of an animal is
eternal as the soul of man. Indeed, use of the word "overwhelming"
too weak a statement. One cannot honestly or intelligently interpr
this passage in Job any other way. Let men presume. God has spok
and the topic is settled.

SPECIAL OFFER

Please read Gary's sequel to this book, **"Cold Noses II, Examining More Evidence"**. With over 200 pages of exciting new ideas and commentary, the author examines every pertinent verse in the Bible that addresses animals as it relates to the afterlife, in a convincing and compassionate way. He also addresses the latest phenomenon fad of "ghost pets" and "signs" and puts them in proper Biblical perspective, at the same time tenderly acknowledging that God does speak to us in our moments of grief. Gary's perspective is unique and thought provoking, but most of all, uplifting and educational. If you want to be spiritually challenged, this book is a must read.

This is a special offer for those who have read "Cold Noses at the Pearly Gates". Instead of the $15.95 store price, your price is only $13.95 and we will pay the shipping and handling. If you order 3 books or more, we will lower that price to only $11 per copy and still pay the shipping and handling.

Send orders to: Cold Noses II
                   P. O. Box 853
                   Manhattan, KS 66502-9998

* * * * * * * * * * * * * *

For re-orders of this book, **"Cold Noses at the Pearly Gates"**, the costs are:

1 copy	$11.00
2 copies	$ 9.50 each
3 or more	$ 8.75 each

Order from the same POB, minus the "II".   Shipping and handling is not charged unless you want books to go to multiple address, in which case the charge is $2.00 per book.

If the author's schedule permits, we can often obtain his autograph and have him write a personal note as you desire. We will not delay the delivery of your order if his schedule has him out of town.

PLEASE VISIT OUR WEBSITE AT www.coldnosesbook.com. The author has written several articles and there are lots of other features intended as helps to those who love animals.